# RE-IMAGINING AFRICA

"Africa Must Innovate Her Way
Out of Poverty"

# BENEDICT KAZORA

# ⅅEDICATION

I dedicate this book to my grandfather's son and that son's grandchild. Mr. Kazora has been my inspiration from day one and remains a great influence to date. Watching him navigate the world of diplomacy and public service offered me great lessons on serving and giving back. It was with this backdrop that I find it my solemn responsibility to also play a similar part in the world that my son, Cameron will inherit. I realized that I can't look far enough in my son's future without looking deep enough into my own past. Life can only be understood by looking at the past but must be lived forward

**********************************

# Introduction

Africa is a continent where people's perception of hopelessness is often overwhelming, and poverty is still at the center of intellectual work and thinking in the continent. So, the narrative of a rising Africa is being challenged.

In the past, ancient worlds were filled with curious explorers who scavenged new lands that were rich in resources, culture, and unique leadership systems. The ancient African civilization was comprised of well-strategized and adequate administrative systems, which enabled them to defend their territories, keeping at bay enslavers and colonizers, meaning they were one of the strongest continents in the world. However, following various failures in the kingdoms and empires, many administrative systems failed. This exposed Africa to slavery and colonization, resulting in a massive loss of power.

There is a philosophy behind every system. Majorly, people's value systems contrast. It is an individualistic idea. One's value system is formed by one's rectitude and iniquity. Africa must take responsibility for herself and look for solutions that will bring the whole continent out of poverty. This is challenging because the continent is not doing well so far. Africa should be able to learn lessons from her past and make sure to not repeat the same mistakes, so that the continent can rise again.

Africa should make efforts to attain financial stability because their economies still retain the same structure that they have had for decades. It should invite investors around the globe to invest in different sectors to reduce the unemployment ratio because underemployment is a serious problem. The education systems in many countries of Africa are broken; they need to find a way to make this system better. They have to unleash the talent of their young people, support them in order to allow them to create, innovate, and lead the way. The government should recognize the strength of women and girls and should support them so they can contribute to the continent.

This book contains 21 lessons that Africa can learn from and implement in order to become a strong continent once again.

\*\*\*\*\*\*\*\*\*\*\*\*\*\*\*\*\*\*\*\*\*\*\*\*\*\*\*\*\*\*\*\*\*\*\*\*

# Contents

Lesson 1: The Great Empires And Kingdoms Of Pre-Colonial And Pre-Slavery Africa ................................................... 1

Lesson 2: Contribution Of Moral Philosophy In Contemporary Economics ................................................... 10

Lesson 3: Why The Us Got It Right? ................................... 20

Lesson 4: Africa Must Stop Reacting And Start Acting ............ 27

Lesson 5: Healthcare Post Covid-19 ................................. 33

Lesson 6: Africa's Covid-19 Solution Lies In Information And Not Isolation ................................................... 40

Lesson 7: Working Women Are A Rising Tide That Lift All Boats ................................................... 47

Lesson 8: Thanks, President Trump For The Travel Ban On African Nations Of Libya, Somalia, Eritrea, Tanzania, Nigeria, And Chad ................................................... 58

Lesson 9: How Artificial Intelligence (Ai) Is Reshaping The Workplace ................................................... 67

Lesson 10: Remittances Are Not Diaspora Investment ............ 70

Lesson 11: Africa Must Innovate Her Way Out Of Poverty - Fourth Industrial Revolution And Africa's Opportunity To Close The Economic Gap ................................................... 83

Lesson 12: The Unbreakable Chain: Blockchain And The Healthcare System ................................................... 93

Lesson 13: Demand & Supply Planning: Solving The Food Security Challenge .................................................................... 97

Lesson 14: The New Realities: Ar & Vr ................................. 101

Lesson 15: Machine Learning - Turning Current Challenges To New Opportunities ................................................................ 104

Lesson 16: Internet Of Things (Iot) ...................................... 107

Lesson 17: Role Of Big Data In Today's Business Environment ................................................................................................ 110

Lesson 18: Artificial Intelligence And Counselling ................. 114

Lesson 19: Emotional Recognition ....................................... 117

Lesson 20: Upstream Thinking ............................................. 119

Lesson 21: Summary ........................................................... 128

Conclusion ......................................................................... 133

# Lesson 1

# THE GREAT EMPIRES AND KINGDOMS OF PRE-COLONIAL AND PRE-SLAVERY AFRICA

**THE LAND OF PUNT:**

The Land of Punt is believed to have been geographically positioned on the Red Sea coast of East Africa. Historical records state that this Kingdom dated back to around 2500 B.C. According to Egyptian historical records, the Land of Punt has been portrayed as a land belonging to gods. The Land of Punt was thought godly by the Egyptians following the inexplicably different fauna and flora make-up of the land. The Ancient Egyptians believed the Land of Punt was rich in ebony trees and wood, high-quality gold, and was filled with spices such as myrrh and exotic animals. Archaeological researchers suppose that during the 15th century, under the reign of Queen Hatshepsut, Egyptian flotillas and large caravans were commissioned to a trade mission to this land. This was evidenced by a discovered papyrus painting, which showed the preparations. Time was of great importance to Ancient Egyptians. It enabled them to plan for cultivation and harvesting times following the yearly cycle of seasons. The astronomers and priests needed correct timing for daily rituals and religious festivals. Hence, the sundial was invented to aid in calculating the correct timing. However, during the night, sundials were functionless as the sun was out of view.

A man named Amenemhat invented the water clock, which enabled accurate timing throughout the day and night. An ancient traveler named Pythagoras, during his visits to Egypt discovered "the-rope sketchers." They were the engineers of time who accurately build the pyramids with the use of a circular rope that had 12 evenly spaced knots. However, the rope was pinned with two of its sides forming an L; a triangle was always formed. Later, as Pythagoras was drawing a 3–4–5 triangle with three squares on all sides, he learned that the areas of the two smaller squares equaled the area of the larger square. Hence, he represented his findings mathematically and the Pythagoras theorem was born.

Ancient Egypt was a land filled with jaw-dropping facts. These Africans developed a book called "*Coming Forth by Day and Night*" presently known as "*Egyptian Book of the Dead*". It was translated from the ancient Egyptian writing to English by Sir Ernest, an Egyptologist. This led to the discovery that the Christian Bible was written by Africans since the writings were dated before the Bible.

**CARTHAGE EMPIRE:**

In the City of Tunis, which happens to be the capital city of Tunisia, there lie a series of ruins. These ruins encompass a rich history of a once-powerful Carthage Empire. History records that this ancient African Empire was so influential to the extent that it rivaled Rome during the Punic Wars. Its influence was felt as far as Spain from North Africa. The Carthage Empire lasted for a long time, estimated to exceed 500 years, and is believed to have started around the 8th or 9th century. It solely began as a settlement for the Phoenicians, however, it evolved into a sea trading empire as it majored in the trade of textiles, gold, copper, and silver. This Empire grew astonishingly into inhabiting five hundred thousand people. It was located in a protected harbor that had a holding capacity of two hundred and twenty ships.

Carthage was well managed and had an insatiable urge to expand its empirical scale. It was this urge for growth that led to conflicts with the Roman Empire. This saw Rome and the Carthage Empire engage in a series of Punic Wars. The first Punic war started in 264 B.C, and the third Punic war ended in 146 B.C that ended by almost completely wiping out the Carthage Empire.

## MALI EMPIRE:

History holds that the ancient Mali Empire is one of the jewels of the African continent. This Empire was widely known all over the world following its hefty indulgence in jewelry. Hence, it flourished in wealth and luxury. So wealthy was this Empire that legends hold that Mali's emperor, Mansa Musa, stopped over in Egypt during the 14th century while on a pilgrimage to Mecca and gave out so much gold to the extent that the gold market prices in Egypt dropped for some years. The Mali Empire is believed to have begun in the 12th century. Its founding ruler, Sundiata Keita, known as the "Lion King," revolted against a king of Sosso

Kingdom, transforming the Sosso's subjects into his newfound governance. The successors of the "Lion King" increased their ruling power over most parts of the Western Africa region. Hence, the Mali Empire grew tremendously in trade.

The main religion in this Empire was Islam, therefore well-designed mosques and Islamic schools filled the Empire. Djenne and Timbuktu were the main cities, whose fame was primarily derived from the elaborate mosques that they harbored. Timbuktu City was home to the Timbuktu Sankore University, which was famously known for having approximately 700,000 manuscripts. Despite its wealth and riches, the Mali Empire gradually died down in the 16th century.

**KINGDOM OF AKSUM:**

Little is known concerning the origin of the Aksum Kingdom. However, history holds that this Kingdom existed during the same period that the Roman Empire did. The Aksum Kingdom had present Eritrea and the northern parts of Ethiopia under its rule, only that the two had different ancient names. History holds that the Kingdom of Aksum was a trading juggernaut as it was heavily involved in the ivory and gold trade with old Europe and other continents. The Kingdom had a uniquely designed architectural style, which entailed the construction of giant obelisks from stone. The written manuscript was the first to be developed in ancient Africa and was known as Ge'ez. The stone build obelisks stood to an astounding height of 100 feet at the time. During the 4th century, Aksum Kingdom stood out by being the first Kingdom, not only in Africa but also in the world, to adopt the Christian religion. This religious step is evident to this date in Ethiopia as the Orthodox Church, despite the fact that the ruler at some later point had denounced it, it remained. The Kingdom enjoyed a military alliance, following the adoption of Christianity with Byzantines.

## KINGDOM OF KUSH:

This Kingdom was of the ancient Nubian Empire and bordered Egypt at its northern side. History holds that the Kush Kingdom lasted for ten centuries as a regional African-based power. The Kush Kingdom is thought to have gained total control in administration after its first a thousand years of existence B.C. This was after it won massive ruling along the River Nile, which is Sudan in the present world.

The Egyptian history records hold that the Kush Kingdom majored in economic activities, which were lucrative and included the trade of ivory, incense, gold, and partly iron. Funny enough, history holds that it was a trading partner as well as having a military rivalry with Egypt, to the extent of ruling Egypt as its 25th Empire. It learned and absorbed many customs from its neighbors. Hence, the Kushite's believed in several Egyptian gods; they practiced mummification of the dead and even constructed pyramids of their making. Currently, the ruins of the ancient Kush Kingdoms boast of more monuments than those in Egypt.

## GREAT ZIMBABWE:

It was thought that the Zimbabwe ruins were once the biblical Queen Sheba's dwellings. However, history and historians are of varied opinion. They believe the Great Zimbabwe ruins were the capital city of an ancient empire, which had functioned from the 13th through to the 15th century — putting at bay all the myths attached to these ruins. The ruins are composed of arranged boulders, granite stone towers, and perimeter walls made of cut granite blocks. The ancient Kingdom is believed to have ruled over the more significant portion of what is presently; Zimbabwe, Mozambique, and finally Botswana. The Kingdom was thought to be wealthy since it was rich in cattle and had a sufficient flow of precious metals. In addition to the resources, it was located near a trading route, which facilitated the flow of the Kingdom's gold to the ever-ready market ports of the Indian Ocean coasts. The Kingdom left little knowledge of its history. However, from the unearthed artifacts, much has been gathered. The Arabian glassware, Chinese pottery goods, and European textiles prove the existence of the profitable once existent mercantile trade. The ancient city of Great Zimbabwe is estimated to have housed over twenty thousand people. The fall of this great ancient city was after it was evacuated, for unknown reasons, during the 15th century.

## SONGHAI EMPIRE:

This ancient African Empire boasts, indisputably, a large area of administration. It is estimated to have been more significant than the area that Western Europe covers in today's world. History holds that the Songhai Empire was formed during the 15th century. It integrated some of the regions that were formerly under the Mali Empire rule. The Empire is run by bureaucratic systems, which divided the massive Empire into sizable provinces administrated by the governors. The economic growth was mostly dependent and came about following the well-thought out trade policies. Songhai Empire experienced its peak under the reign of the devoted King Muhammad I Askia. This King found new lands by conquest. He fixed an alliance with the Muslim Caliph of Egypt as well as building many Islamic schooling facilities in Timbuktu. Following the devotion of King Muhammad I Askia, the Songhai Empire rose to great heights and became the most powerful Empire in the world at the time. However, in the late 15th century, it lost power control following long civil wars. It also suffered from tensions from within, which left the Kingdom vulnerable to invasion by Morocco's Sultan, therefore marking its end.

\*\*\*\*\*\*\*\*\*\*\*\*\*\*\*\*\*\*\*\*\*\*\*\*\*\*\*\*\*\*\*\*\*\*\*\*

## ALMORAVIDS CONQUEST OF SPAIN

Almoravids were the Islamic Berbers dynasty, which was centered in Northern Africa, presently the modern Morocco, parts of Algeria and the Western Sahara region. However, the need to expand the Almoravids Empire of western Africa was motivated by religious competition since the Almoravids wanted to spread the Islamic tradition in the Northern Africa regions, which were dominated by Islamic Spain and Christianity.

Toledo was the capital city of the Taifa Kingdom of Al-Andalus or the Moorish republic of Al-Andalus. Due to its stable economic activities and well-organized administrations the kingdom thrived drastically, enabling it to conquer its territorial enemies like the Castilian army and Moroccans, hence founding Marrakech as its capital. Consequently, in 1085, the Toledo city fell to the siege by King Afonso VI of Castile spurred the Reconquista, the Christian conquest of Muslim Spain. However, this was a crucial moment in the struggle between Christians and Muslims in the Iberian Peninsula.

The Almovids dynasty ruler Yahya ibn Ibrahim formed and ruled his kingdom basing on the Islamic religious believes. Ibrahim formed the empire from a religious movement in the Western Maghreb at the end of the 11th century. Ethnically, this kingdom was more Berber than Arab. They conquered Morocco and established Marrakech as the capital. However, when Toledo fell in 1085, Yusuf ibn Tashufin of the Almoravids received a plea from the Moorish leaders in Spain to help repel Christian armies. In 1086, the Almoravids army defeated the Castilian and Aragonese armies at the battle of Sagrajas. This gave them additional control over an empire stretching more than three thousand kilometers from north to south of their empire. Further, as a result of economically stable empire and well-organized armies, the Almoravids were able to completely seize control of Al-Andalus in year 1090.

The dynasty fell at the zenith of its power. A rebellion led by Ibn Tumart (Masmuda rebellion) killed the last ruler of Almoravids in Marrakesh in 1147. Consequently, Almohad Caliphate replaced them as the ruling dynasty and exerted their power both in Morocco and Al-Andalus

# Lesson 2

# CONTRIBUTION OF MORAL PHILOSOPHY IN CONTEMPORARY ECONOMICS

Philosophy is segmented into six major branches out of which Ethics or Moral philosophy is a significant part. Moral philosophy is based on suggesting and systematizing the notion of right and wrong conduct. A chain of command of values that every moral being has reflected in their decisions. Majorly, people's value systems contrast. It is an individualistic idea. One's value system is formed by one's rectitude and iniquity. There are nine regular economic qualities that individuals consider while assessing the economic philosophies like, productivity, speed, dependability, usability, adaptability, status, stylish intrigue, feeling, and cost.

## ROLE OF PHILOSOPHERS IN CURRENT ECONOMY:

The ideas of philosophers are used for the value system of current economics which were presented previously in the 18th century and earlier.

Adam Smith is named as the founding father of moral economics. He studied *"Moral Philosophy"* at the *"University of Glasgow"*. Later, he became the head of Moral Philosophy as a lecturer in the university. His first published book was *"The Theory of Moral Sentiments*". He had ideas of fewer trade barriers, free economies with less government regulation, and lower taxes. Physiocrats helped in shaping his economic views. In 10 years, Smith wrote his most renowned work "*The Wealth of Nations*" which discovered why some of the countries prosper while others languish in poverty. It is one of the most influential writings of the last millennium. His two published books together comprised a towering achievement in the history of western thought.

Smith's theory is implemented in current economics, which is the concept of "*Gross Domestic Product*" (GDP) and for his theory of compensating wage differentials. Today, the world has become increasingly integrated by trade, finance, and commerce.

Economics is the study of wealth, tangible material goods, and changes in wealth mean economic development. Big thinkers like Adam Smith and Karl Marx consider capitalism and socialism as two strengths and weaknesses of economic systems. Adam Smith brought a brand-new sort of theory about economics to explain to people how nations can become rich and powerful. Capitalism is the key concept of a good economic system and it is the reason why capitalism is good. The success of capitalism is also called an invisible hand, which people cannot point with but it is something that balances out people's and producer's interests while keeping the reality in mind that competition is out there. The consumer is benefited by having so many choices and low prices of products. This is a huge benefit to capitalism.

The invisible hand has a key impact on a community such as resources or factors of production land labor and capital owners will shift to where society needs them. The second key point which is impacted is the recycling of goods for continually moving into the economy. This makes an efficient economic system. Capitalism is a self-regulating system so Smith argued for no or very little government involvement. When everything in goods can be settled by competition and morals, then there is no need for the government to create strict rules for it.

In his book *"Moral Sentiments"*, Smith called conscience an impartial spectator and observed himself so that people can interpret the behavior, and he realized that one is accountable for his actions. He also helped in driving the move from land-based wealth to wealth created from assembly-line production methods. His invisible hand theory is applied to free markets and capitalism through supply and demand. His contribution is also seen through the economic development theory in which economic growth takes place through the principle of division of labor. He led the *"Laissez-faire"* (let you do) policy.

Utilitarianism is an ethical theory founded by *"Jeremy Bentham"* by the principle of utility which adheres to the belief that an act is virtuous if it provokes happiness or it is a vice if it tends to cause agony to the greatest number of people. *"John Stuart Mill"* developed and publicized this concept. Utilitarianism is something to think about in terms of what is in the best interest of a great number of people. Bentham introduced the *"Felicific Calculus"*. It is also called utility calculus or hedonistic calculus. It includes intensity, duration, certainty, propinquity, purity, and extent. The felicific calculus formula is the formula of balance between happiness and pain, but John Stuart Mill said that the measure of pleasure cannot be calculated. In the current economy, people apply utilitarianism by analyzing whether the benefits of action outweigh the harm of that action.

Some other utilitarian contributors include:

- Cooper, Anthony Ashley Inquiry Concerning Virtue or Merit, in Characteristics of Men, Manners, Opinions, and Times.

- Cumberland, Richard, 1672. De Legibus Naturae Disquisitio, Philosophica, and London. A Treatise of the Laws of Nature.

- Gay, John, 1731. A Dissertation Concerning the Fundamental Principle and Immediate Criterion of Virtue in Frances King. An Essay on the Origin of Evil.

- Hutcheson, Francis, 1725. An Inquiry into the Original of people Ideas of Beauty and Virtue.

In business decision making, after people add up all the positives and negatives for all stakeholders, if the results are positive overall, the decision is ethical.

"*Auguste Comte*" is the founder of sociology and positivism, which emphasizes empirical observations and says that "*only real concrete things can be considered which knowledge is gained through five senses*". The ambition of Comte's positive philosophy was to reorganize society along with new scientific principles.

There are three fundamental elements of society in Comte's law;

- The first is intellectual knowledge.

- Second is the political government of the state.

- The third one is an artistic, philosophical, and economic civilization that is generated by the first two.

His ordering is the reversal of Marx's ordering as for Marx, economic and industrial factors are the roots of other factors while Comte's concept generates artistic superstructure which justifies the economic status quo. For Marx, the solution is going to be a revolutionary change in the material distribution of the means of production in society, whereas Comte and his positivism have the ambition to change the political order and civilization by providing a deeper intellectual unity to it. Comte's positivism had two primary effects. A new science of social facts was introduced and named sociology and the principle of unity of the science of society was envisaged under one heading.

The "*Keynesian Economics*" by John Maynard Keynes was used to refer to the fact that optimal economic performance and prevention of economic slumps could be achieved by influencing aggregate demand through activist stabilization and economic intervention policies by the government. Scarcity is a major economic problem in which there is a gap between limited resources and limitless wants.

It is the condition in which individuals are forced to make choices among available alternatives. Resources available for production are land, labor, and capital. Scarcity and resource allocation put economics at the center of many studies. Making the best decision with a variety of choices is efficient but, in this case, people do not always choose wisely.

Keynes argued to stimulate economic crisis by two approaches:

- A reduction in interest rates (monetary policy).

- Government investment in infrastructure (fiscal policy).

During a recession, the government may employ expansionary fiscal policy by lowering tax rates to increase aggregate demand and fuel economic growth.

By the courtesy of Karl Marx, communism became a heated debate which swayed the realization of the stateless society where we are all equal. Today the global disparity between rich and poor is startling. He already predicted the global financial crisis by capitalism in which the bourgeoisie or entrepreneurs who control the industries, and the proletariat or laborers whose work changes crude products into significant financial merchandise, are only two classes of society among which one is privileged and the other is deprived of deserving rewards.

He also predicted that capitalism will lead to boom-and-bust economics. His concept was to morally appreciate the manufacturer by crediting him for the result of his labor instead of just receiving some money in return for one's work. It makes a human being utterly expendable. He was not in favor of selling one's credit along with hard work which he had done to make something productive out of raw material. He believed that capitalist companies had shrunk the allowance of workers in order to attain a large profit.

Karl Marx believed in the labor theory of value to explain relative differences in market prices. This theory stated that the value of a produced economic good can be measured objectively by the average number of labor-hours required to produce it.

Implicitly, in putting this forward as truth, this amounts to a belief in economic growth and progress as the path to a stage in the future which is more than common quality to an ecstasy. This implicit economic belief is quietly ignoring standard goods/money-making methods of analysis of markets and other economic issues. The range of short-run costs that financial analysis normally has nothing to do with, is wide. As part of the necessary price of progress, any good citizen having rights in the nation should be ready to take for such costs that are in the way of religion and that are kept away from economic calculations. Religion hinders the pace of economic progress which is manipulated by scientific methods as well as being inaugurated by intellectuals and philosophers as it provokes faith over science and rationality.

Many of the economists and environmentalists in the world support the belief systems and associated values, though often implicitly. Depending on the theory, people often surprisingly agree that economics and environmentalism are religions, but this is not a fact as religion is based on utmost faith and mere belief.

## AFRICA GROWING WHILE SHRINKING:

According to the "*National Bureau of Economic Research*" one-half of Africans live below the poverty line. In sub-Saharan Africa, GDP per capita is now less than it was in 1974, having declined over 11 percent. While the rest of the world's economy grew at an annual rate of close to 2 percent from 1960 to 2002, growth performance in Africa has been dismal. Morocco is one of the continent's commercial hubs. It was Africa's leading fish producer in 2014 and hopes to make fishing one of the key pillars of its economy. Tourism is another key industry. "The *Ivory Coasts*" is the world's number one producer of cocoa and cashew nuts. It is also Africa's largest producer of bananas. Ivory Coast is also the second-largest producer of palm oil and third for cotton or coffee. Ghana has seen poverty halved in 20 years with exports of gold, cocoa, and oil. Nigeria is Africa's largest economy and the largest oil producer on the continent. Agriculture, information technology, commerce, and services are also driving the continent's economic expansion. South Africa remains the most industrialized country on the continent due to the exportation of national resources like gold, platinum, and diamonds. The Johannesburg stock exchange is the largest by market capitalization. Kenya is known for its technology hub on the growing base of subsidiaries of firms like Intel, Google, and Microsoft.

The contemporary environment of global finance was previously predicted by theories of moral philosophy. Moreover, contributions are made by moral philosophy, scientific techniques, and mathematical formulas derived for the solutions for economic problems and are applied to the current value system of economics where Smith's contributions remain some of the most significant. Being called the *'Father of Economics'* perfectly suits an economist like Adam Smith as he advocated for a free market system of economics, as well as introducing:

- Law of self-interest so people work for their own good.

- Law of competition which forces people to make a better product.

- Lowest possible price to meet demand in a market economy.

Smith proposed that a nation's wealth should be judged by its total production and commerce. Today, this is known as the gross domestic product (GDP) where GDP is an accurate indicator of the size of an economy and the GDP growth rate is probably the single best indicator of economic growth, while GDP per capita has a close correlation with the trend in living standards over time.

*************************************

# Lesson 3

## WHY THE US GOT IT RIGHT?

Every three years the Organization for Economic Co-operation and Development (OECD) carries out the Program for International Student Assessment (PISA). This assessment measures what more than 600,000, 15-year-old students have learned in math, reading, and science. Similar to many years, in 2019 the US scored below average in mathematics. The US students' scores were similar to those of Australia, Germany, New Zealand, Sweden, and the United Kingdom in at least two subjects. On receiving this latest report, the US Secretary for Education Betsy DeVos said, "*The bottom line is there has not been a single study that shows American education is improving enough.* " DeVos went on further to acknowledge that "*we are being outpaced not only by our global competitors like China and Russia but also by countries like Estonia, Finland, and Canada*". This might explain why in recent years, we have seen a push for Science Technology Engineering and Math (STEM).

With growing years, it was believed that science was the way to go if one wanted to change the world. Innovation was firmly linked to science and technology. The methodical approach to life's problems has proven valuable but only to a certain point. However, a good mix of arts with the sciences in the African education system should be seriously considered as the way to move forward. The real issue lies in the minimization of the role of arts while sciences are amplified. The real solution is placing more emphasis on the arts.

## Where Africa's Gap Is:

While sciences have been revered on the continent and viewed as the only means for innovation, the US case has proved this philosophy to be inaccurate. The US has mastered that and kept her leadership in technology and innovation despite poor performance in math, this has been due to the arts. To take a brief journey back in time, it is believed that writing, artificial intelligence, or the internet was simply the most important innovation of all time. This technology was primarily designed to record accounts so fast that it exploded into a means of informing and recording. Also, it allows for expression of all of the political, social, cultural, historical, and most interestingly private thoughts, as well as actions of all walks of society so subsequently, the invention of the printing press allowed for literacy to be readily expanded. This allowed people to share large amounts of information quickly and in huge numbers. Imagine a world without newspapers or libraries today.

## CASE STUDIES- IMAGINATION DECIDES EVERYTHING:

## ERIC NSHIMIYE:

Eric Nshimiye is among one of the best minds I have ever known. Working on his doctorate in Aerospace Engineering and

Mechanical Engineering from Notre Damme and Purdue Universities; Eric is also the church pianist. Eric has been mentioned as the best Agriculture student in the whole of Uganda during the ordinary level exam in his year. While he had a distinction in agriculture, he also had the same in chemistry and physics. He is a professional photographer and the IPU Podcast producer. With two patents (Aerospace and Automotive) to his name, Eric remains among one of the most talented people in the world.

## MARK ZUCKERBERG:

Almost half of 18- to 34-year-olds check Facebook as soon as they wake up. Studies have shown that Facebook is even more addictive than cigarettes. According to the Pew Research Center, 74% of US Facebook users visit the site daily. This company has been valued at $677B today and is at the core, more about psychology than science. Mark Zuckerberg was a Harvard psychology major that took many computer sciences classes. It is the art side that features in the more prominent aspects of Facebook. Studies have connected Facebook to the brain's reward center known as the nucleus accumbent. This is the area that processes rewarding feelings like money and sex. When people's Facebook "*likes*" were fed into an algorithm, one was able to predict whether someone was white or African American with 95% accuracy, whether they were a gay male with 88% accuracy, and even identified participants as a Democrat or Republican with 85% accuracy. The '*likes*' list predicted gender with 93% accuracy and age could be reliably determined 75% of the time. During his talk at Birmingham Young University, Mr. Zuckerberg said Facebook is *"as much psychology and sociology as it is technology."*

## JAMES ALLISON:

In the science world, many know James as the father of immune checkpoint blockade, an entirely new way of treating cancer that is yielding unprecedented results. His drug ipilimumab (Yervoy) is the first-ever to improve survival for patients with advanced melanoma.

However, when he is not in the lab, James and his fellow immunologists spread across multiple institutions and companies in the US forming a band called *"The Check Points"*. This band was named after the work that won James Allison the 2018 Nobel Prize. James Allison is an expert harmonica player and has even played with the famous Willie Nelson.

## LEONARDO DA VINCI:

Leonardo played off the strengths of both the logical and the creative parts of the brain. As much as he was a superb artist, painter, and sculptor, he was also an inventor. In the 1960s, the Mona Lisa painting went on a tour where it was given an insurance valuation of $100 million. In a recent interview, the founder of Faber novel, Stephane Distingue suggested that France should sell Leonardo's Mona Lisa for €50 billion (£44.7 billion) in order to cover the COVID-19 costs. This value is equal to more than Africa's bottom 17 countries GDP combined.

A last supper is an event chronicled in all four of the Gospels. This event marked the first celebration of the Eucharist, a ritual still performed today. This previously undiscovered piece was priced at $15.8M by French auction house Tajan. On the other hand, Leonardo is believed to have conceptually invented the parachute, armored tank, machine gun, and a helicopter. Leonardo also greatly advanced the state of knowledge in the fields of Anatomy, Astronomy, Civil Engineering, Optics, and the study of water (hydrodynamics).

## STEVE JOBS:

Steve Jobs remains one of the most exciting innovators of our times. As of January 2020, Apple was worth $1.3 trillion which is 66% of the whole of Africa's GDP. Even though Apple is known for its technological advancements, Steve attributes his and Apple's success to the arts. Before Apple, Steve transformed Pixar into a movie-making powerhouse. Since the release of Toy Story 25 years ago, every one of their movies has become a commercial success averaging $550M per movie.

During the launch of the iPad 2, Jobs said *"It is in Apple's DNA that technology alone is not enough, it is technology married with liberal arts, married with the humanities, that yields us the results that make our heart sing."* In his 2005 commencement speech at Stanford University, Steve noted that it was his sitting in on Palladino's calligraphy class at Reed College that inspired the elegance for which the Apple computers are renowned. He said, *"If*

*I had never dropped out, I would have never dropped in on this calligraphy class, and personal computers might not have the wonderful typography that they do. Of course, it was impossible to connect the dots looking forward when I was in college. But it was very, very clear looking backward ten years later."*

As far back as 1878, the winner of the first Nobel prize in Chemistry Henricus pointed out that most famous scientists did have artistic predispositions. He proceeded to cite examples such as *'Isaac Newton'* the prolific painter and *'Galileo Galilei'* the poet. It all made sense to him because science was creative at the core. Anyone can make an unthinking observation, but he remarked that it takes a tremendous amount of imagination to conjure up theories and the tests to prove them.

## Science Without Conscience Is but the Ruin of the Soul:

The founder of Alibaba, Jack Ma stated that the Chinese education system teaches very well but does not unleash the student's complete intelligence, yet allows them to experiment and enjoy while learning. This completely captures Africa's education system at its core. It is perhaps the right time for the African education system to engage scientists with issues of ethics and responsibility. This can be done by requiring them to take classes in arts and humanities to allow them to be more engaged in discussions of morals and values. Fareed Zakaria put it best when he said that *"a lot of what makes us succeed in life is not related to science and technology"*. It is things like how to think, one's communication skills, and the ability to place things in context. English and Philosophy teach us skills that remain consistently useful in the ever-changing technology-driven economy. The truth is, anyone can make a $25 pair of sneakers somewhere in a factory in Vietnam. The real challenge is how to sell that pair of sneakers for $350. That calls for branding, marketing design, and advertisement. This is true for cars, cellphones, and just about anything else. To achieve this, you need more than just science and technology.

## Mastering How Technology Interacts with Humans:

Despite lagging other superpowers in mathematics and science, the US has remained the most innovative country with the largest economy. African education experts must look closely at what is causing this. Simply put, it is a broad education system that fosters critical thinking and creativity. The same emphasis which is placed on Physics and Math should be placed on English and Psychology. At the end of the day, innovations are no longer merely a technical issue, instead, it now requires a deeper understanding of how people and societies work for their needs and wants. Africa will not catch up with the western world by only making more affordable technology rather by perpetually reimagining how that technology interacts with human beings. It is high time Makerere University offers degrees such as a Master of Science in Music and Technology.

\*\*\*\*\*\*\*\*\*\*\*\*\*\*\*\*\*\*\*\*\*\*\*\*\*\*\*\*\*\*\*\*\*\*

# Lesson 4

# AFRICA MUST STOP REACTING AND START ACTING

*"Urban Design Is the Antidote for The Continent's Next Health Crisis"*

## Extraordinary Times Require Extraordinary Responses:

On May 15th, 2020 The Guardian published an interesting article titled "*Africa facing a quarter of a billion coronavirus cases, Who Predicts*". The report approximated 220 million Africans based on that article. Now, while the western media predicted doom and gloom for the youngest continent on earth, data seems to be painting a completely different picture during this pandemic. Africa is partly to blame for not taking control of her narrative and not shedding enough light on her success stories. It was not until the former British barrister and daughter of a Ghanaian lady, Afua Hirsch, that Africa's positive COVID-19 stories surfaced. She highlighted Senegalese handling of COVID-19 that makes the likes of Italy and England envious. This small West African nation took a textbook approach to handle the COVID-19 pandemic. It was the methodical and decisive approach that led to only 30 deaths. The Senegalese government displayed compassion never seen anywhere yet. Each of the bereaved family members were visited and consoled by Macky Sall's government. Senegal was also able to invent a $1 COVID-19 test kit which works the same way as the $308 England version.

Another untold story is that of Ghana. Ghana focused more on "pool testing" in which multiple blood samples are tested and then followed up as individual tests only if a positive result is found. Today, the *"World Health Organization"* is studying Ghana's approach. As the results of Africa's response to COVID-19 gain more visibility, the most powerful nations will need to study what went right among smaller and less powerful ones. By March 2020, Ghana had carried out more COVID-19 tests than the US states of Montana, Hawaii, Wyoming, and Vermont combined.

While Africa's response to COVID-19 is noteworthy, the tendency to react rather than acting still prevails. Granted, Africa was fortunate this time to experience the COVID-19 tragedy after many other nations. This gave her time to prepare and plan based on the available information. Africa must not let the worst blight go to waste.

**Looking Back to See Forward:**

Looking back to London in 1854, the largest city at the time. London was hit hard by a terrible cholera outbreak. Many of the scientists believed this disease was airborne. However, there was a lack of evidence to support this theory. It was Dr. Snow who, through investigative means, linked the outbreak to contaminated water well in Soho, which was the epicenter. It was the results of this work and the desire to avoid a repeat that led to what we know today as the modern sewage system. A similar story can be told about the tuberculosis epidemic in New York in the early 20th century. This epidemic paved the way for improved public transit systems and housing regulations. Comparably, the 2003 SARS outbreak led to Singapore and Hong Kong's upgrade of the medical infrastructure to create systems that can map the disease.

## Urbanization and Social Distancing:

Africa's urbanization rate of 3.5% per year is the fastest in the world. The "*United Nations*" reports that by 2050 more than two-thirds of the global population will live in urban areas. It was Dr. Rudolf Virchow that founded the term "*Social Medicine*". This discipline seeks to implement social care through understanding how social and economic conditions impact health, disease, the practice of medicine, and fostering conditions in which this understanding can lead to a healthier society. Studies have also shown that with proper urban design, a society can increase life expectancy. Neighborhoods with lower income and education levels often lack sufficient green space, sidewalks, bike routes, adequate housing, which in turn, is contributing to lower physical activity levels and higher rates of chronic diseases such as obesity and heart disease.

## The Future of African Cities:

It is against this backdrop that Africa must seize this moment and take action to cope with the new realities. Most African countries are presently and aggressively working to realize their visions of becoming middle-income economies. People have glanced at Tanzania's Vision 2025, Kenya's vision 2030, Rwanda's vision 2035, and many others. Also, we are yet to see plans that will deal with the next epidemic or pandemic. Better yet, plans that will help the continent control epidemics.

As early as 400 BC, Hippocrates theorized that poor physical environments, like bad air and water, caused illness and disease, and believed that going to areas with fresh air and water were essential to health. The now common word quarantine, which means restricting the movement of people or goods, is rooted in the Italian word Quaranta Giorni which means "*Forty Days*". This is a reference to preventative measures taken in Venice during the middle ages to stop the spread of the bubonic plague. Ships arriving from areas affected by the "*Black Death*" were required to anchor for 40 days before the crew could disembark. It is now clearer than ever before that the most critical response to epidemics and pandemics is more a physical one than a biological one.

## Africa's Cities Must Be Designed to Be Medical:

Africa must glance at the past to design cities of the future by looking at the spatial response to disease control. The focus must be placed on building cities that are resilient, self-reliant, and that improve health outcomes. Architecture and urban design should be designed to be medical to be able to control the spread of the next epidemic.

The Mayor of Paris, Hildago plans to build the "*15-Minute City*". This will enable residents to access every basic need from work, health, shopping, and culture within 15 minutes from their doorstep. This modification is projected to cut down on air pollution that kills 3,000 people a year primarily caused by car traffic. This approach also saves work hours lost in transportation to and from work. Hildago has also introduced free water fountains throughout Paris, enabling people to have access to free, clean water. He's also created a plastic bottle recycling machine near to these fountains, meaning people are encouraged to reuse and recycle. This is not unique to Paris; Barcelona (Spain), Portland (Oregon), Melbourne (Australia), and many other cities around the world are modifying urban planning to make cities healthier. One of the key components of these healthy cities are parks that serve as the lungs of our cities. A great example is "*Vienna's Parc de la Distance*". This park will have numerous routes divided by 90-centimeter-wide hedges to maintain a safe physical distance between its visitors. Arranging the paths in a fingerprint-shaped swirl pattern creates many routes that can be used simultaneously. Each of the red-granite gravel paths through the park would be around 600 meters long and circulate visitors from the edge of the park to the center, where fountains would be located, and back round. The public health effects of urban design have become increasingly apparent over the past decades. Life expectancy can be increased or decreased depending on the part of town people live in. The COVID-19 pandemic is a blessing in disguise. Taking the lessons from this pandemic will enable the continent to prepare for the next one. It is time to examine the future of the cities in correlation to the healthy lifestyles of the population the continent desires to succeed. Let future city designers have that at the very core. Africa must act to avoid reacting once again in the future.

********************************

# Lesson 5

## HEALTHCARE POST COVID-19

*"Prevention Is Better Than Cure"*

- It was the spring of hope and the winter of despair.

- The cost of treating Coronavirus is $34,927.43.

- Texas loses about $85 billion for every $1 drop in oil prices.

- In 2017, if the US cut the administrative costs to match those of Canada, the US would have saved more than $600 billion in that year alone.

When looking at the world today compared to a couple of months ago, we are reminded of the famous author "Charles Dicken's 1859" book named *"A Tale of Two Cities"*. While comparing life between London and Paris at the time, Charles noted *"It was the best of times, it was the worst of times, it was the age of wisdom, it was the age of foolishness, it was the epoch of belief, it was the epoch of incredulity, it was the season of light, it was the season of darkness, it was the spring of hope, it was the winter of despair"*. With more than 1.55 million COVID-19 cases and over 86,000 deaths in the US alone, we certainly might be heading to a winter of despair.

According to a recent "*Time Magazine Article*", the cost of treating Coronavirus is $34,927.43. In 2018 the US alone spent a total of $3.5 trillion on healthcare and is projected to reach 6.2 trillion by 2028. That expenditure is more than the 5th largest economy in the world (United Kingdom). As if this is not enough, healthcare spending is projected to grow at 0.8% faster than the GDP.

Three score years ago, healthcare was 5% of the US economy. Today, it is 17.7% of the total GDP. This was all Pre-COVID 19.

States are beginning to open and the talk of seeking herd immunity is more prevalent in some circles. If one in five Americans were to get infected, it has estimates of up to $163 billion in indirect cost. Besides the direct cost, there are a plethora of indirect costs as well. COVID-19 led to a sudden drop in demand for oil for example. The New York Times reported that the state of New York could lose up to $15 billion in taxes from tourism and business travel alone. Forbes reported that the cancellation of the Cactus League season will cause the Phoenix area about $100 million in losses of economic impact.

## We Live Like Poor People, But We Die Like Rich People:

Granted, these are unique times, to put it mildly. However, the healthcare concerns remain at top of most American minds. To look at what causes this and what can be done, first off examine a good example of healthcare that works and that is not a burden to the populous. Cuba's expenditure on health per capita is $971 while that of the US is $10,224. In Cuba, healthcare is considered a human right for all citizens which makes healthcare a real national priority. As a result, Cuba's life expectancy is higher than that of the US (72.5 years' vs 71.9 years). Health workers in Cuba have managed to eradicate polio, tuberculosis, typhoid, and diphtheria. Additionally, the rate of infant mortality in Cuba has been lower than in the Boston neighborhood with prestigious hospitals like Harvard's Brigham and Women's. As a result of this and other impressive metrics, Cubans like to say, "*We live like poor people, but we die like rich people.*" Cuba has a surfeit of doctors and doctors per capital with ratios almost thrice those of the US, through what they now refer to as doctor diplomacy, Cuban doctors have stepped up to the aid of others at every opportunity. From earthquakes in Indonesia and Pakistan, the Cholera outbreak in Haiti, the Ebola epidemic in West Africa, and most recently in Europe to fight COVID-19. Most people know Cuba as a huge sugar and tobacco exporter but leasing her healthcare professionals to foreign governments brings Cuba almost $11 billion each year. This makes this industry more lucrative than tourism in Cuba.

## How Do the Cubans Do It?

If a doctor gives someone's family a complete annual checkup, he will go further to examine and record living conditions to find out if there is anything that can endanger their health and that of any family member. Well, this is what happens in Cuba. This proactive slant has proven to be cost-effective and yields amazing results. It is from the results of these checkups that doctors classify different residents based on their risk profile. The target here is to stop people from getting sick in the first place. As one doctor put it, *"It is cheaper to treat hypertension by exercise than do a coronary bypass"*.

## What Makes US Healthcare So Expensive?

Since 2008, average family premiums have increased 55 percent, twice as fast as worker's earnings (26%) and three times as fast as inflation (17%). Administrative costs are frequently cited as a cause for excess medical spending. A 2020 publication on Annals of Internal Medicine cites that administrative costs in the US account for about 34 % of the total healthcare expenditure. This was twice that of Canada. One of the main drivers of this is the huge array of usage and billing requirements from multiple payers. A study showed that in 2017 if the US cut the administrative costs to match those of Canada, the US would have saved more than $600 billion in that year alone. This is almost equivalent to the Illinois GDP.

- **DRUG COSTS ARE RISING**

Abiraterone is a drug used to treat metastatic prostate cancer. Now, this drug does not cure but merely extends life by an average of four months. The cheapest this drug can be sold at is $10,000 per month. Johnson & Johnson, who make this drug, justify the cost by saying the funds are needed to pay for research and development of future drugs. Novartis' Zolgensma for childhood disorder has recently been approved by the FDA and will cost

$2.125 million per patient. This, as you can now tell, explains the fact that Americans spend more than $500 billion on drugs alone per year which is about 16% of the total healthcare expenditure per year. This January, Congressman Jared Huffman put it best when he said, "*Prescription drug prices are killing people right now*". The US House Committee reported that US drug prices are nearly four times higher than the combined average in 11 other countries in Europe and Scandinavia as well as Japan and Australia.

- **EXORBITANT HOSPITAL COSTS**

Hospital care accounts for 33% of the nation's healthcare costs. Between 2007 and 2014, prices for inpatient and outpatient hospital care rose much faster than physician prices, according to a 2019 study in Health Affairs. US prices for surgical procedures in hospitals greatly exceed those of other countries. A typical angioplasty to open a blocked blood vessel, for example, costs $6,390 in the Netherlands, $7,370 in Switzerland, and $32,230 in the United States. A 'C.T Scan' costs $97 in Canada and $896 in the US while an MRI scan costs only $450 in Canada and $1,420 in the US.

## Suggested Solutions:

At this rate, the US healthcare cost will soon be a leading cause of death. To remain affordable in the future it is important to use the vast resources to emulate the Cuba model. This prevention-centric approach has already proven to be cost-effective while yielding a higher quality of life. In addition to that, it has come to a time where it is necessary that we look at other price control measures taken by other industries such as the airlines, energy, and agriculture to circumvent the ever-increasing costs.

## Healthcare Futures Market:

In the 1980s amidst shortages and volatile pricing, oil futures were created. This later inadvertently stabilized the oil market due to the predictable pricing. A futures contract is simply a contract between a buyer (for example an airline) and a seller (an oil company) for goods at a future date at a price negotiated and fixed today. It is a form of hedging where both parties remove the uncertainty of tomorrow's prices. This has been critical in the airline industry because the cost of fuel accounts for almost 20% of the airlines' expense. A great example of the advantage of futures was evident in the 2000s when Southwest Airlines had locked in the fuel price at $51 a barrel for several years while its competitors were paying more than $90 a barrel. The cost of healthcare has risen steadily and inexorably for the last 50 years.

A disease like diabetes can be used as an example in healthcare. The American Diabetes Association's March 2018 report showed that the total cost of diabetes rose from $245 billion in 2012 to $327 billion in 2017. This same report suggested that those diagnosed have medical expenditures approximately 2.3 times higher than what expenditures would be in the absence of diabetes. The cost of treating diabetes today is higher than the cost of oil. After adjusting for inflation, the economic costs of diabetes increased by 26% from 2012 to 2017 due to the increased prevalence of diabetes, and the increased cost per person with diabetes.

All known future markets are in industries that are organized vertically by specific products. This allows investment in specific crops like soybeans or oats. However, the healthcare industry is still organized horizontally. The US has only three insulin manufacturers serving the US market; Eli Lilly, Novo Nordisk, and Sanofi. However, they all make other drugs as well. This poses a challenge in the investment of a specific disease in the healthcare sector. Changes in the suggested industry serve as precursors for the investment in healthcare's future. This new approach will not only stabilize costs of treatment but will in the long run save patients billions as they battle these chronic and incurable diseases.

\*\*\*\*\*\*\*\*\*\*\*\*\*\*\*\*\*\*\*\*\*\*\*\*\*\*\*\*\*\*\*\*\*\*\*\*

# Lesson 6

## AFRICA'S COVID-19 SOLUTION LIES IN INFORMATION AND NOT ISOLATION

### A Look at Hubei Vs New York:

- The black death pandemic is estimated to have killed up to 60% of Europe, which was an estimate of 450 million people in the 14th century.

- Today a virus can travel first class on KLM to Africa and infect millions.

- In Taiwan, when an infected person leaves their home or turns the phone off, the police and local authority will be alerted and the person will be visited within 15 minutes.

- The Co-100 app shares when the person tested positive, their nationality, gender, and age.

### Africa's Advantage in the War with COVID-19:

The richer nations have been the first to succumb to the COVID-19 scourge. This is primarily owed to the business and tourism between China and the west. Africa has benefited from late infections and has the advantage of lessons learned from the earlier victims and how other nations have dealt with it. Examining the Asian and European reactions to this pandemic in Africa is primed to implement the best of both worlds. To this end, the critical soldiers in this unique battle against the pathogens, are the data scientists in concert with the healthcare workers armed with data. This approach will save the continent millions of lives, jobs, and the continent's vulnerable economy.

## Tale of Two Localities:

## Hubei & New York:

With only 404 COVID-19 (0.07% of the population) cases, Singapore has proven more adept at handling this pandemic than New York. Despite a greater distance from the epicenter (Hubei Province), New York has 2.3 times more cases compared to Singapore, relative to the population. With 81,281 cases out of 1.4 billion people, it is hard to deny that China got it right.

The Hubei province with a population of 60M people had 67,801 cases. This infection rate of 0.1% remains less than in New York. Wuhan, the COVID-19 epicenter had about two-thirds of all China's cases, is about to lift the lid and resume life as normal. While the western world is grappling with this pandemic, it seems there are many lessons to learn from the east.

## People Have Been Down This Road Before:

During the 14th to 19th century, the world dealt with the *"Black Death"*. This was a disease that was spread by body lice and started in Italy, spreading across Europe to France, Spain, Portugal, Scotland, and Scandinavia among others. This pandemic is estimated to have killed up to 60% of Europe, which was an estimate of 450 million people in the 14th century.

Like COVID-19 today, the smallpox pandemic was equally class-blind, killing the rich and poor alike. This plague is estimated to have decimated close to 30 million Mexicans by 1568 which was way before the arrival of Hernan Cortes. Despite the Spaniards having a superior army, the microscopically (smallpox) that the 'Cortes' army unwillingly brought from Europe helped take down the Aztec empire. This disease spread along trade routes in Asia, Africa, and Europe, eventually reaching the Americas. Smallpox is estimated to have killed 300 million people in the 20th century alone. It is also estimated that the fatality rate was 30% of those infected.

Wherever it began, the 1918 flu pandemic lasted just 15 months but was the deadliest disease outbreak in human history, killing between 50 million and 100 million people worldwide, according to the most widely cited analysis. The effect of the flu pandemic was so severe that the average life span in the US was depressed by 10 years.

## It Is Information, Not Isolation:

Without airplanes or cruise ships, we have seen diseases spreading from eastern to western Europe and across continents. This means that closing borders are not a permanent solution. Germany took in about 50 Italian COVID-19 patients to help with the treatment. Germany's gesture speaks to the power of collaboration and sharing of information that has proven to be the best weapon against these pathogens. Sweden has not closed its borders or schools. Neither has it closed non-essential businesses or banned gatherings of more than two people, like the U.K, and Germany. Sweden has taken the unorthodox approach of simply informing and trusting the citizens.

Sweden's 10 million-strong population has reported 3,700 cases and only 110 deaths, while New York reports about ten times the rates of death and infections while the population difference is only double. This phenomenon further shows that isolation is not a true solution.

Over the years people have seen doctors win the battle against pathogens one time too many. The secret lies in the fact that while pathogens rely on blind mutations, the doctors have been armed with the powerful scientific analysis born of information. Third world countries have always struggled to deal with the likes of *"Ebola"* due to the non-data driven approach. This present danger posed by COVID-19 presents the third world with a chance to examine novel ways of fighting pandemics and epidemics. This will term the information-driven approach as the Asia approach.

It has been seen again that the Asian nations of China, Singapore, Taiwan, and others have proven more efficient at handling the pandemic. Africa's political philosophies happen to be more aligned with those of Asia than those of the west. In a world where a virus can travel first class on KLM to Africa and infect millions, information becomes the only tool available to combat this. The US strongly adheres to privacy laws and that makes the collection of pertinent data much more difficult. Perhaps it is time to examine the modification of these laws during such gruesome times and whether people are willing to temporarily trade privacy for life.

## Data Is the Most Lethal Ammunition in This War:

In Beijing, the "*Beijing Cares*" app has been integrated into the permeating "*WeChat*" app. People under quarantine are made to input their daily temperature and health status into the app. When the isolation period is over, a "*Healthy Status*" page is generated, which users can flash at buildings and malls to gain entry. The Chinese government also releases details about patients' travel history - via text messages on the mobile phone and state-managed websites - so the public can avoid places where the virus was once active.

South Korea took more aggressive steps by deploying an innovative system using data such as surveillance camera footage and credit card transactions of confirmed COVID-19 patients to recreate their movements. Max Kim of the "*MIT Technology Review*" reported that the Ministry of the interior and safety use their Corona-100m (Co100) app, which allows those who have been ordered not to leave home to stay in contact with caseworkers and report on their progress. The app will also use GPS to keep track of their location to make sure they are not breaking their quarantine. Additionally, the app allows users to see how close they are to places that COVID-19 patients have visited before testing positive. As if that is not enough, the app also shares when the person tested positive, their nationality, gender, and age.

Taiwan went further to implement mobile phone electronic fencing. This location tracking platform ensures that those quarantined remain at home. The primary intent here is to ensure those infected are not running around spreading the virus. When one leaves their home or turns the phone off so they can't be tracked, the police and local authority will be alerted, and the person will be visited within 15 minutes. Officials also call twice a day to ensure the phone is not left at home by the infected person. The fact remains that the virus does not travel from place to place airborne, but humans carry the virus from one place to another.

## Can People Sacrifice Their Privacy to Save Their Lives?

The mentioned slants would run afoul of privacy laws in the west. However, this is perhaps the most ideal time for African countries to come up with the *"Infection Protection Act"* akin to the German version being modified to deal with COVID-19. MTN Group has close to 244 million subscribers while Vodacom has over 110 million. Altogether, close to 750 million people in Africa have cellphones. The solution to the war with COVID-19 and future pandemics hinges on leveraging data and technology to complement doctors' efforts. The World Health Organization (WHO), Director-General Tedros Ghebreyesus said *"The steps*

*China took to fight the virus at its epicenter were a good way of stopping its spread.*" Africa must act fast and swiftly because this is ultimately a sprint and not a marathon.

**********************************

# Lesson 7

# WORKING WOMEN ARE A RISING TIDE THAT LIFT ALL BOATS

*"It is Time to Release the Girl Power in All Its Forms"*

In 2013 George Zimmerman was acquitted of murder in the death of '*Trayvon Martin*'. Many were shocked by this verdict, but this was going to start a movement that would have a huge impact on the political and social space in the US. Later, Chicago's Anita Alvarez failed to charge police officers who shot and killed at least 68 people. The "*Black Lives Matter*" movement helped to ensure Anita was not re-elected for the "*Cook County*" prosecutor position. In Florida, Angela Corey, the state attorney, failed to convict Trayvon Martin's killer and instead prosecuted Marissa Alexander, a black woman who did not harm anyone when she fired a warning shot at her abusive ex-husband. *"Black Lives Matter"* was the first US movement that leveraged the internet as a mass mobilization device. It was on this success that the *#MeToo* and many other movements were built upon.

The "*Black Lives Matter*" movement influenced the democrats to restructure their national platform to include issues such as criminal justice and reform. This movement was shown to have led to the election of Black leftist organizers to public offices, such as activist "*Chokwe Lumumba*" to be elected as the mayor of "*Jackson,*

*Mississippi*". From July 2013, through May 1, 2018, the *"BlackLivesMatter"* hashtag had been used nearly 30 million times on Twitter, an average of 17,002 times per day, according to a "Pew Research Center" analysis of public tweets using *"Crimson Hexagon software"*. Pew Research compared hashtags between January 1, 2013, and May 1, 2018. The #BlackLivesMatter hashtag was used 1.3 million times on Twitter which was 500,000 more than the #MeToo and Trump's #MAGA hashtags. This huge movement was started by three young ladies (all under the ages of 35 years); Patrisse Khan-Cullors, Alicia Garza, and Opal Tometi.

In 2020 alone, almost 41% of the entire continent of Africa will be holding major elections. This background needs to focus on the role of women in the economic development agenda. Women make up about 50% of the total planets' population. In some countries such as Ukraine, El Salvador, Portugal, Hong Kong, and Russia there are more women than men. But this population ratio is not reflected in politics, board rooms, science, and technology.

**Legislative Limitation:**

It took more than 140 years after America's independence to allow women to vote via the 19th amendment of the US constitution. Before this, married women could not own property and had no legal claim to any money they might earn. To this day, women's' rights in the US constitution are not explicitly guaranteed. About 48 years ago, Congress passed the *"Equal Rights*

*Amendment*" but this was never ratified. The 14th amendment ratified in 1868 does have the equal protection clause but women's rights remain unguaranteed to this day.

Prof. Rohlinger of Florida State University suggested that the reason the equal rights amendment has not been ratified by all states includes fears of the disruption of the traditional gender roles including child-rearing. Additionally, Prof, Rohlinger believes that women will lose their exemption from the draft. "*Theodosia Nshala of Women's Legal Aid Center*" in Tanzania mentioned that both sexes have equal rights to land ownership in large part owing to the Village Land Act in 1999. Customary laws on the other hand still prevent women and girls from inheriting land from their spouses and parents.

## Social Hindrances:

Gender inequality arises at its most embryonic form when women do not have total control over when they are ready to be mothers. Globally, 40% of pregnancies were unintended. 50% of these unintended pregnancies ended in abortions, 12% in miscarriages, and 38% in unplanned births. Women with unintended pregnancies often have to stop working or studying and become economically dependent rather than independent. Research from the "*Harvard Department of Global Health*" predicts that 80,000 women will leave the workforce in 2020 alone due to unintended pregnancies. As a consequence, for every woman forced to leave the workforce due to unintended pregnancy, the human capital index drops.

It has been documented that women's access to employment, business opportunities, financial resources, and economic empowerment is linked to improvements in reproductive health. An increase in the use of contraceptives and access to high quality sexual and reproductive health services, longer birth intervals, and planned pregnancies allows higher labor force participation by women, which improves the economic status of families and creates a robust workforce driving the economy.

Studies have also shown that women are inherently disadvantaged by cultural and psychological factors. Female entrepreneurs often lack access to capital which encumbers business growth. Women have proven to be risk-averse and a leadership gap exists between men and women, especially in the African context. *"Eyerusalem Siba of Africa Growth Initiative"* suggested the use of different capital-based, training-based, and gender-based interventions will likely help close the gap. Some of these interventions include lessons on the creation of business plans, networking, the establishment of virtual stores, and access to new market components.

## World War 1:

Before World War One, most work was done by men, and women remained primarily responsible for taking care of the children and the home. When the war began and most men went to fight, a gap was created in the workspace. Soon the production of munition almost came to a halt while the need increased. It did not take long before there was a need to employ women in these factories.

By 1917, munition factories, which at the time had primarily women employees, were producing 80% of the weapons and shells used by the British Army. Women risked their lives by exposing themselves to the trinitrotoluene used in making explosives. This exposure led to the demise of about 400 women during World War One. By the end of this war, the women's employment rate had risen from around 23% to about 46%.

In some pockets, we still see the gap wider than ever. In Africa, women form the majority in the informal sector but there is only one woman out of every three people in the formal sector. International *"Finance Corporation"* also reports that women's ownership of *"Small and Medium-Sized Enterprises"* (SME's) account for only 33%. This is critical because SME's are the engine of growth. American Express published the 2017 *"State of Women-Owned Business Report"*, showing that women-owned businesses employ about 9 million people in the US and generate $1.7 trillion in revenues.

Some have argued that increasing women's participation in the workforce will increase the demand for labor which will, in turn, lower the wages. It is suggested that if women join the workforce due to an increase in opportunities then wages increase. This is due to the shift in labor participation will be caused by an increase in demand. Furthermore, an increase in women's participation in the labor force might lead to a replacement of less productive men, thus increased productivity. Prof. Amanda Weinstein noted that as women surpassed men in obtaining college degrees in 1982, they likely raised overall skill levels and also introduced complementary skills.

## Economically Empowering Women:

## Is Not a Zero-Sum Game

In 2015, Prime Minister Justin Trudeau was asked about his decision to have a cabinet that was 50% female, he responded succinctly by saying *"Because it is 2015"*. Unlike a few decades ago, Forbes 2019 edition of the most powerful women in politics highlighted the fact that the mentioned women oversee $54 trillion in GDP and more than 3.5 billion people. Additionally, a report by Jonathan Woetzel et al, suggests that if women's participation in the economy is equated to that of men, we can potentially add $28 trillion to the global GDP by the year 2025.

In recognizing this, Norway's Board Membership Rule requires women to make up 40% of the publicly listed boards. Short of this, companies risk dissolution. The Economist reported that in the five years following this rule, more than a dozen countries set similar quotas. In countries like Belgium, France, and Italy, penalties also include dissolution or even ban from remunerating directors together. Ahunna Eziakonwa of the

*"United Nations Development Program"* revealed that since 2010, Sub-Saharan African economies lose $95billion a year because of the gender gap. S&P Global mentioned that, if U.S. companies hired and promoted women at the same rate as countries like Norway, the economy can grow by 8%. S&P Global's analysis also shows that German's GDP would be 11% bigger while those of France and Japan would be 16% and 14% bigger respectively.

## Closing the Gap for Good:

To truly empower women, policymakers need to address a couple of major constraints among others. Firstly, people need to migrate away from the cultural beliefs about gender and power. Secondly, people need to overturn the aspiration barriers that keep women in a constant subordinate state along with the aforementioned internalized constraints.

Many women have overcome general impediments and remain pivotal to the future of our societies and the globe in general. As people celebrate women today, it is important to shed some light on some of these remarkable women that have shaped the world of business, politics, science, and technology.

- **Marie Curie** was a physicist and chemist whose radioactivity research laid the foundation for modern nuclear science, from X-rays to radiotherapy for treating cancer. She was the first woman to win the '*Nobel Prize*', and the first person to win two '*Nobel Prizes*' in different sciences.

- **Wangari Maathai** was a Kenyan scholar and environmental activist. She founded the pioneering Green Belt Movement in 1977, which encourages people, particularly women, to plant trees to combat environmental degradation. Her holistic approach eventually led her to link environmental responsibility to political struggles of governance, human rights, and peace. She was awarded the '*Nobel Peace Prize*' in 2004.

- **Katherine Johnson,** known as Katherine Goble, was an American mathematician whose calculations of orbital mechanics as a "*NASA*" employee were critical to the success of the first and subsequent US crewed spaceflights. During her 35-year career at "*NASA*" and its predecessor, she earned a reputation for mastering complex manual calculations and helped pioneer the use of computers to perform tasks.

- **Bibi Titi Mohamed** was one of the leaders of the "*Tanzanian Nationalist Movement*". Born into a Muslim merchant family, she entered politics in 1955, becoming the first female member of the "*Tanganyika African National Union*" (TANU), an independent party led by Julius Nyerere. As a singer and a musician in the community dancing groups (Ngoma) of Dar-es-Salaam, she helped to recruit more than six thousand women for the (TANU).

- **Margaret Thatcher** changed the face of modern British politics. She started her political career at *Oxford University* where she was president of the *"Conservative Association"*. In 1959, she won the parliamentary seat in Finchley and became *"Margaret Thatcher"* (MP). But she made history in 1975 when she became a leader of the *"Conservative Party"* - one of the two major political parties in the UK - and later, in 1979, the first female British Prime Minister. She had some pretty radical views and even earned herself the nickname The Iron Lady.

- **Rosa Parks** - In 1955, Rosa Parks, an African American living in *'Montgomery, Alabama'*, challenged the racial segregation that existed in parts of the US by refusing to give up her seat on a bus so that a white person could sit down. Her protest was supported by many other African Americans and sparked the civil rights movement which, in the 1960s, eventually won equal rights. Four years after her death in 2005, Barack Obama became the first African-American US president.

- **Coco Chanel** - opened her first shop in the early 1900s, starting by designing hats. She soon turned her attention to clothes too and, by the 1920s, launched her first perfume. Ever heard of the saying the *'little black dress'*, also known as the (LBD)? Almost 100 years after it was first created, Chanel No 5 is still probably the world's most famous perfume.

- **Huda Shaarawi** - was a pioneer and Egyptian feminist leader and nationalist. She helped to organize *Mubarrat Muhammad Ali*, a women's social service organization in 1909, and the

Intellectual Association of Egyptian Women in 1914. Her feminist activism was complemented by her involvement in Egypt's nationalist struggle. She established the *'Egyptian Feminist'* Union in 1923, was the founding president of the 'Arab Feminist Union', and spoke widely on women's issues and concerns throughout the Arab world and Europe.

- **Dr. Hayat Sindi** - Scientist and First Female Saudi Assembly Member. Apart from being the first Saudi Arabian woman to be accepted by Cambridge University for a Ph.D. in Biotechnology, Dr. Hayat is also amongst the first women to be a part of the *"Consultative Assembly of Saudi Arabia"*, has made major contributions to the medical field, and has been ranked the 19th most influential Arab in the world by Arabian Business.

- **Angela Merkel** became the first female Chancellor of Germany in 2005 and is serving her fourth term. Merkel remains the de facto leader of Europe, leading the region's largest economy after steering Germany through a financial crisis and back to growth. Her leadership is marked by her steely reserve, from standing up to *"Donald Trump"* to allowing more than a million Syrian refugees into Germany. She has a Ph.D. in quantum chemistry and is fluent in Russian.

- **Elite troops** of women soldiers contributed to the military power of the "Kingdom of Dahomey" in the eighteenth and nineteenth centuries. Admired in their country and feared by their adversaries, these formidable warriors never fled from danger. The troops were dissolved following the fall of Behanzin (Gbêhanzin), the last King of Dahomey, during French colonial expansion at the end of the nineteenth century.

Today, 56% of college students are women. For the first time, in the last year women aged 25 and older now account for more than half of the college-educated workforce (50.2%). It is time to re-examine the policies, our long-held cultural norms, and to reconsider the role of a woman in society. Barriers to success for girls need to be removed so they too can realize their fullest potential. Like the quote of the 22-year-old Pakistani girl Nobel Prize Laureate, Malala Yousafzai - *"I raise my voice—not so that I can shout, but so that those without a voice can be heard. We cannot all succeed when half of us is held back."*

\*\*\*\*\*\*\*\*\*\*\*\*\*\*\*\*\*\*\*\*\*\*\*\*\*\*\*\*\*\*\*\*\*\*\*\*\*

# Lesson 8

## THANKS, PRESIDENT TRUMP FOR THE TRAVEL BAN ON AFRICAN NATIONS OF LIBYA, SOMALIA, ERITREA, TANZANIA, NIGERIA, AND CHAD

**Questions to Ponder Upon:**

The origin of the name "Africa" stems from the words used by the Phoenicians, Greeks, and Romans. Keywords include the Egyptian word, "*Afru-ika*" meaning motherland, the Greek word "aphrike meaning "*without cold*" as well as "*aprica*" a Latin word meaning Sunny. Olduvai Gorge in Tanzania holds evidence of the earliest human ancestors. Africa is a continent with a rich history, most beautiful cultures, and a highly educated populous. 25% of all the languages in the entire universe are spoken on this one continent as noted Jared Diamond in his 1997 Pulitzer Prize-winning book, "*Guns, Germs, and Steel*".

"*Why are we having all these people from shithole countries come here*" -Trump in January 2018. These remarks included some African countries. On January 31st, 2020 President Trump extended his travel ban to include Eritrea, Nigeria, Sudan, and Tanzania. With a population of 1.3 billion, Africa's GDP is $2.19 trillion, while that of the USA is at a staggering $21.44 trillion. France, the United Kingdom, India, Germany, and Japan all have higher GDP than all of Africa combined. Norway's GDP is per capita is $81,485, while that of Burundi's is $310. It takes 24 African nations to aggregate $1 trillion in GDP, far more than any other region in the world. Most of Europe has a single trade zone, named the European Union, while Africa has a 16-trade zone. It takes 3 hours or less to reach European countries aggregating 70% of Europe's GDP and 8 hours for Latin America but 15 hours for a comparable trip in Africa. It does cost less to ship a car from Paris to Lagos than from Accra to Lagos. Acha Leke Saf and Yeboah-Amankwah in their Harvard Business Review article titled *"Africa: A Crucible of Creativity"* highlighted that Africa has more than 400 companies whose revenue exceeds $1 billion. Africa has all the precursors to be the world's largest economy to attain its deserving dignity.

## Possible Explanation:

A National Geographic report suggested that by 1850, Africa's population would have been 50 million instead of 25 million. The report goes further to suggest that slavery contributed to the colonization and exploration of the continent. It is suggested that as a result, infrastructure and communities were damaged, and this made Africa vulnerable to colonialism. If it had not been for the slaves in America, the cost of building industry and agriculture would have been much higher, therefore the standard of living would be much lower. Today's western culture is a hybrid of that of African and local customs. This ranges from food to music. While acknowledging the impact of slavery on the continent, it is fair to highlight that the westerners did not settle in large numbers. However, they were successful in extracting the continent's wealth, first the human capital (through slavery), then diamonds, copper, and rubber.

Africa is able to host 60% of the world's arable land that has not been cultivated, but still imports $35billion worth of food annually. This figure is projected to increase to $110 billion by 2025 if nothing is done. Even more mind-boggling is the fact that Africa exports raw material out of the continent and turns around to import the same products processed. Africa is essentially contributing to its poverty by exporting jobs in the process. A 2018 *"Africa Development Bank"* report noted that Brazil transformed its tropical Cerrados into a $54 billion food industry in just two decades. Certainly, this feat required innovative soil and crop management programs, as well as new agriculture technologies. Africa's Savannah is more than double that of Brazil and employing a few of the mentioned techniques will certainly make the continent a net exporter of agricultural products.

The challenge remains one of the extractive natures of Africa's political and economic systems. The *"World Economic Forum"* reports this as part of the reason why the impact of foreign aid is never seen trickling down to most citizens. The aid, in turn, ends up being a tool to continue enslaving the citizens and at times eroding the continent's culture and identity with the attached strings. In his book *"Confessions of an Economic Hitman"*, John Perkins elucidated the tricks that are behind the so-called loans.

Karen McVeigh's article in *"The Guardian"* shared a sad finding that in 2015, Africa received $32 billion in loans but paid $18 billion in debt interest alone. As Perkins highlighted such loans are not structured with Africa's interest in mind. This coupled with poor leadership means Africa finds itself in a perpetual race to end poverty. Political evolution is what is believed to differentiate Africa from the West. The West has proven to host economic and political systems that allow for inclusion and equal opportunities. Botswana is a perfect example of the effects of good governance. 50 years ago, Botswana was a very poor African country, yet today has a GDP per capita of $8,258. This African nation is richer than the European nations of Bulgaria, Serbia Albania, and Ukraine. This is primarily due to good governance and its handling of the natural resource (diamond) wealth. A good economic institution protects private property rights, enforcement of contracts is predictable and controls inflation.

Thabo Mbeki's Report of the *"High-Level Panel"* on Illicit Financial flows from Africa reports that for the past 50 years, Africa has lost over $1.2 to 1.4trillion dollars to illicit flows. This was equal to the financial assistance given to the continent in the same period. While these transactions are usually dismissed as a result of pure corruption, Mbeki's report showed that 65% of these illicit flows were commercial transactions. Some of how this is achieved is through trade mis-invoicing. Multinational corporations have used technics referred to as base erosion and profit shifting, which are essential forms of tax evasion from high tax countries to low tax locations. Multinationals decide how much profit to allocate to different parts of the same company operating in different countries, and then determine how much tax to pay to each government. Meanwhile, embezzlement and bribery constitute only 3% of these illicit outflows.

African countries have done a wonderful job building modern road systems. However, only 33% of Africans live within 2 kilometers of a paved road that is usable all year round. The cost of travel within the continent is ungodly. Travel costs in Africa are between five and eight times that of Brazil or Vietnam. The Economist reported that despite Africa being home to a fifth of the world's population, the continent accounts for only 4% of the global electric use. About 70 percent of the population are shown to have no access to electricity.

## Urbanization, A Challenge, And Opportunities:

McKinsey & Company notes that Africa's development is directly correlated with urbanization. While this introduces infrastructural challenges in major cities, it also implies a growing consumer market. Between 2010 and 2020, there was a bigger growth in sales of food and beverages in Cairo than in Brasilia and Delhi. This can be best captured in the fact that today, Nairobi's per capita income is three times that of Kenya. Those who live in Lagos are now earning twice the amount of the nation's average. In the oil-rich nation of Angola, the capital city of Luanda accounts for 45 percent of the nation's consumption. While this is exciting for the consumer market, the right development policies need to be put in place so growth can be equally dispersed.

## The Way Forward- the African Continental Free Trade Area Agreement (AfCFTA):

Africa is not resourced as poor by any means. Africa is the richest continent on earth. South Africa's potential mineral wealth is estimated at $2.5 trillion. If fully realized, this would put South Africa ahead of Italy and Brazil as the 8th largest economy in the world right behind France. Simultaneously, the *Democratic Republic of the*

*Congo's*" mineral wealth is estimated to be worth $24 trillion. The Congo does not only have the potential to be the richest nation on the planet, but richer than the European Union. Numerous other stunning finds exist about the potential of the continent. However, Africa must trade its way to its fullest potential. With a staggering population of 1.3 billion people, Africa is already populated enough to trade amongst themselves, without the need to trade with Europe or the rest of the world, so Africa's intra-trade is paramount.

The share of intra-Africa exports has increased over the years to about 17% presently. However, this is still very low compared to other regions. Europe is at 69% and Asia at 59%. The "*AfCFTA*" is believed to be the answer to most intra-Africa trade-related issues. This agreement will certainly unlock the continent's economic potential if properly executed. The mere removal of tariffs is expected to boost the continental intra-trade by $50 billion to $70 billion by the year 2040.

To enhance intra-trade, a key impediment that needs to be removed are the tariff-related costs. According to the Abuja treaty, all regional economic communities should have established a common external tariff within customs unions and fully functional free trade agreements by end of 2017. The Economic Community of "The *Central African States*" (ECCAS) has the lowest intra-regional trade. This region posts the lowest intra-regional trade in the continent and for this to change, these tariffs should essentially be wiped away.

Non-tariff barriers also pose an equally challenging obstacle to intra-trading. These broadly include policies that reduce the cost of transactions that stem from custom administrations, documents required, and enhanced transport infrastructure. These policies are needed to reduce transaction costs as well as those that create an enabling environment for trade which includes reduced bureaucracy and corruption.

## Efforts Being Made:

International companies such as Maersk, Imperial Logistics, and a few others have played a key role in facilitating intercontinental trade. Between 2005 and 2016 the mentioned companies helped increase intra-Africa trade from $30billion to $64 billion.

Another industry that is playing a key role in connecting the continent is the airline industry. As of 2019 Ethiopia Airlines flies to 37 countries in Africa alone, leading the way. Royal Air Maroc, Air Cote d'Ivoire, and Rwanda Air are leading the continent in the economic integration efforts.

Africa may be lacking in hard power, but the continent should take control of its soft power. Very few countries have leveraged the power and impact of branding. Mauritius's GDP per capita is more than that of Bulgaria or that Equatorial Guinea is richer than Mexico. Talent and capital are increasingly mobile and can have a huge impact on the economy. America is not just a nation but an idea. In 2018 about 23 million people applied for the green card lottery which is given to only 55,000 people a year. Very few of these millions try to make it to the US because they have not done a cost-benefit analysis of the key factors. The power of the American dream and the iconography of the Statue of Liberty mean something. They have value far beyond feel-good expressions of patriotism. They represent America as something to strive for, as an expression of hopes and dreams for a better life, as a fulfillment of a quest for ultimate safety, prosperity, and liberty. African nations need rebranding. Rarely, the *"Ugandan inventor Brian Turyabagye"* has created a biomedical smart jacket that can diagnose pneumonia, a disease that is responsible for 16% of deaths of children under the age of 5. *"Square Kilometer Array"* (SKA) in South Africa, which once completed, is set to be the world's largest telescope that will allow people to see deeper into space. *"Nigeria's*

*Osh Agabi"* has created a device that fuses live neurons from mice stem cells into a silicon chip for the first time. The device can be used to detect explosives and cancer cells. These examples are endless.

Africa indeed should take the travel bans as an opportunity to look inward and seek out its deep inner capabilities. The above issues highlighted are not difficult to resolve if African leaders place their hearts in the right place. With Africa's median age of 19, the continent has the energy, human capital, and vigor to allow the continent to realize its fullest potential as the biggest economy in the world. All precursors are present.

As people strive to realize Africa's dream, it is important not to lose sight of the health of their children, the quality of their education, or the joy of their play. Let the world know of the beauty of her poetry, the intelligence of their vibrant and rich public debates. The world ought to know more about the wit, courage, wisdom, and compassion of Africans. It is the continental collective effort that will organize her citizens and bring forth the best of her skills and energies. This is a challenge that the continent must accept needs to be achieved and is unwilling to postpone.

********************************

# Lesson 9

## HOW ARTIFICIAL INTELLIGENCE (AI) IS RESHAPING THE WORKPLACE

Smart technologies are not only changing homes, they are also edging the way into their various ventures and are disturbing the work environment. *"Artificial Intelligence"* (AI) can improve profitability, proficiency, and precision over an association. As (AI) takes on a greater amount of the work people do, ceaseless learning and an eagerness to grow new skills will probably be a necessity for each worker to keep their job. Artificial intelligence appears will be instrumental in changing and upgrading the advanced work environment. Since work processes upgraded by *"Machine Learning"* (ML), 'AI' will significantly change how people work, conveying incredible experiences for representatives and clients alike.

**Work Gets Faster:**

Artificial Intelligence is reliant on processing force and information. As the two expand, the development of 'AI' will develop exponentially. Advances in 'AI' will prompt work processes that convey increasingly engaged results that are progressively effective, quicker, and progressively controlled. While it is difficult to anticipate precisely what the territory of 'AI' will be in 10 years, these patterns ought to straightforwardly impact regions identified with assembling, social insurance, and security.

## Computerization:

As people progressively anticipate fast workers in the commercial center and the work environment, computerization innovation evacuates dreary errands occupying significant time that could be better spent. Chabot's are appearing in the working environment that can be utilized to respond to basic inquiries, convey diversion to help the day, and give tokens of organization occasions or significant achievements. Chabot's are as of now being utilized to lead worker fulfillment overviews.

## The Combined Workforce:

Different cooperation stages take into account the simple development of what is becoming known as the 'Mixed Workforce'. This is the mix of full-time representatives, low maintenance, independent, and experts. These work plans require adaptability in how and when individuals convey. Tools like Slack, Trello, and G-Suite permit everybody dealing with a similar task to convey and team up continuously. The mentioned software helps to assemble long haul, dependable connections between all partners.

## Secure Information Sharing:

As the working environment develops, the Intranet normally advances with it. Organizations are depending all the more vigorously on their Intranet as an available, secure approach to do everything from sharing data to characterizing organization culture. The Intranet is the place that straightforwardness can be accomplished, with all representatives approaching the data they need and use regardless of where they are.

With regards to testing new advances, numerous organizations have worries about security, life span, and what will most successfully improve productivity and nearby representative fulfillment. The Intranet is the place more organizations are going to use for preliminary new advancements, transparently examine them, and to realize what is and is not working for them. Artificial Intelligence has the extraordinary capacity to ceaselessly gain from and emphasize the information it gathers and moves organizations with the open doors it guarantees. The more information gathered and dissected, the more impressive the machine becomes, and the better people can work closely with these machines.

\*\*\*\*\*\*\*\*\*\*\*\*\*\*\*\*\*\*\*\*\*\*\*\*\*\*\*\*\*\*\*\*\*\*\*

# Lesson 10

# REMITTANCES ARE NOT DIASPORA INVESTMENT

The definition of Diaspora is made by G. Scheffer: *"Modern Diasporas are ethnic minority groups of migrant origins residing and acting in host countries but maintaining strong sentimental and material links with their countries of origin, their homelands."* The term Diaspora comes from the Greek words *"to sow"* and *"over"*, as in the scattering of seed, and for them, it meant the *"seeding"* of Greek colonies in distant lands.

Remittances are funds sent by immigrants to their home countries for various uses, including paying school fees for a relative, covering healthcare costs for the family as well as activities such as building homes to retire. The major driving forces include insurance, investment, and strategic incentives. A report titled, *"Leveraging Economic Migration for Development"* noted that in 2018, the number of international migrants and refugees was estimated to be 266 million persons, of whom 240 million (90%) were economic migrants. The same report highlighted that women made up the majority of the numbers, with the exception of Africa and Asia. Between the years 2000 and 2018, the share of immigrants as a percent of the global population increased from 2.8% to 3.5%. The 2019 report is not available as of this book, but according to the *"World Economic Forum"*, the 2019 global remittances are projected to be a remarkable $715Billion. The 2019 projections have the following countries leading: India ($82.2B), China ($70.3B), Mexico ($38.7B), the Philippines ($35.1B), and Egypt ($26.4B).

## The Africa Diaspora Context:

The remittances discussion, especially in the Africa context, is often misconstrued. People place almost exclusive emphasis on the flow of money from Europe and the Americas into Africa. Global reports rarely speak to the amount of funds Tanzanians in Kenya send home or that Malawians in Ethiopia send back to Malawi. About two out of every three migrants from Sub-Sahara Africa go to neighboring countries. Only 41 percent of emigrants from East Africa, 24 percent from West Africa, 39 percent from Central Africa, and 28 percent from Southern Africa, end up outside Africa. Consider the intra-continental flow, remittances in Africa hit the $85Billion mark in 2018. If the African Diaspora was a country, it would be the 9th largest economy on the continent just behind Ethiopia with a GDP of $90.97 billion.

The 2018 remittances were more than foreign direct investment in the same year ($46B). Quartz Africa reported that Nigeria's 2017 revenue from oil was $20B while the remittances in the same year were $22B. A more interesting observation is that remittances are more stable than all other sources of foreign exchange. Some economists have theorized that remittances can improve nations' creditworthiness. Additionally, they spur spending in sectors such as education and healthcare. Recent findings have shown that Ethiopian households that received remittances are less likely to sell off productive assets such as livestock amidst hardships such as famine. With overwhelming dependence on foreign aid, it is perhaps time for the African governments to turn to the Diaspora for economic development.

## Removing the Remittances Bottlenecks:

*"High transaction fees are cutting into remittances, which are a lifeline for millions of Africans,"* said Gaiv Tata, the World Bank's director for finance and private sector for Africa. To that end, the most pressing issue with remittances today is the exorbitant cost of sending money. The global average of remitting $200 is about 7%, Asia boasts of the lowest average of 5%. Meanwhile, Sub-Sahara Africa is as high as 9.4%. This is typically owed to the fees on the sender and recipient intermediaries as well as the exchange rate margins. In 2017, the total cost of sending remittances was about $30Billion. To put this in perspective, the requested foreign assistance funds by the USA for 2020 is $32.3B. This cost of sending money can build the Mombasa-Nairobi railway (cost $3.2B) about ten times over. *"Sustainable Development Goal"* (SDG) 10.7 has a target of 3% by 2030.

## What causes sending money to Africa to be so expensive?

One reason for such high costs is the limited market competition for cross-border payments. *"Massimo Cirasino"*, a senior World Bank economist suggested that opening up the remittance market to competition and giving better information to consumers could bring remittance prices down. He says that Governments in both sending and receiving countries (in Africa and elsewhere) should discourage exclusive agreements between providers of remittance services (such as commercial banks, post offices, credit and savings cooperatives, microfinance institutions, and mobile money transfer services) and international money transfer agencies, which keep costs high. A recent survey showed that 81% of post offices in Sub-Sahara Africa are located outside three of the largest cities. It is these locations where 80% of Africans reside. On the contrary, mainstream commercial banks tend to be concentrated primarily in bigger cities.

A World Bank report *"Leveraging Migration for Africa-Remittances Skills, and Investments"* noted that providing information on available remittance channels, maintaining databases of the prices charged, and promoting the financial literacy of prospective migrants can strengthen competition in the market. Over the long term, financial development should reduce remittance costs by increasing access to financial services in rural areas and poor communities and should reduce the costs of opening bank accounts.

There is also a loss through converting currencies, not to mention fees and time spent waiting for transfer approvals. Another World Bank study found that fees average 7.09 percent of the amount sent. One of the proposed solutions is the use of bitcoin for these transactions. Blockchain platforms can reduce fees and transfer money. A 5% reduction can add $16 billion a year back to the continents' economy.

Governments can support this process by improving their telecommunications infrastructure, harmonizing banking and telecommunications regulations to enable mainstream African banks to participate in mobile money transfers and to an extent consistent with public safety that simplify anti-money laundering and combating the financing of terrorism (AML-CFT) regulations for small-value transfers, which would facilitate mobile-to-mobile cross-border transactions. Before the activation of the AML-CFT, it was estimated that $2 to 4 trillion dollars were used to finance illicit activities. While this slowed down the funding of illicit activities, it also presents a bottleneck in the remittances process.

In a nutshell, Governments and policymakers should encourage competition and fully exploit the potential of the domestic remittance market. Examples of this include the 'African Development Bank', who work with African governments to introduce policies and measures that will attract remittance flows, and the launch in January 2019 of PRIME (Platform for Remittances, Investments and Migrants' Entrepreneurship in

Africa). PRIME aims to reduce the cost of remittances and increase its impact across Africa.

## Calling Remittances Diaspora Investment in Countries of Origin Is a Misnomer:

African Diaspora has purported that remittances to their countries of origin are a form of investment and demand special recognition to that end. Most remittances are sent directly to the family for private and personal use. Local governments might experience peripheral gains from a Burundian sending money to treat his mother. But if his mother was in Bolivia, that is where the funds would be remitted, so the act of sending money is not a patriotic one, rather a personal one. A Kenyan in Dallas is building a house in his homeland to use when he retires, so does the local Kenyan in Nyahururu. These acts have been misrepresented as investments for far too long.

## Diaspora Public Partnerships (DPP):

In April 1998, India conducted underground nuclear tests known as the Pokhran-II test. As a result, in May of 1998, the US issued sanctions on India. Shortly after the sanctions were imposed, the Indian government turned to the Indian Diaspora as a source of funding by launching the sale of a 5-year bond guaranteed by the State Bank of India. This bond, dubbed the *"Resurgent India Bond"*, was set up to counter the impact of the sanctions impressed upon India. Furthermore, this bond was made more attractive by setting the interest at 2 percent higher than the US bond market.

India launched an aggressive marketing campaign for the bonds in the US and Europe leading to 3 Billion dollars in just two weeks. This unprecedented fit was evidence enough that the Diaspora can serve as a viable alternative source of funding to native countries. $22 Billion, almost half of the Sub-Saharan African remittances, goes to Nigeria. If just 10% of the remittances were converted into investments, it would relieve the Nigerian government from foreign aid with endless strings attached. The 340KM standard gauge railroad in Ghana will cost $2.2 billion, which is 10% of the Nigerian remittances for the year. Nigerians in Diaspora can fund the Ghanaian standard gauge railroad in a matter of months.

## What is a Diaspora Bond?

A country simply issues foreign currency debt targeting the Diaspora. The intended outcome here is that the country benefits from a patriotic dividend that offers lower pricing. Given the example of India, this shows how much funding instruments are crisis resilient. On the Diaspora side, this is an opportunity to contribute to the nation's development. Governments can potentially enhance access to international capital markets by issuing bonds securitized by future remittance inflows. Some scholars believed that Diaspora bonds can improve a country's sovereign credit rating.

## A Creative Diaspora Investment Platform- Accounts Receivables and Purchasing Orders:

Accounts receivable (AR) is the balance of money due to a firm for goods or services delivered or used but not yet paid for by customers. Accounts receivables are listed on the balance sheet as a current asset. 'AR' is any amount of money owed by customers for purchases made on credit. The most common lengths of time to pay the accounts receivable is between net 30 and net 60. Imagine, John Doe delivered $1,000 worth of eggs to Hyatt Regency Hotel in Addis Ababa. This transaction is visible and part of a 'Diaspora Investment Platform'. This online platform has four key elements. Each component is heavily vetted before admission to the platform.

1. **Diaspora** (investor)
2. **Small enterprise (the egg vendor).** Typically, too small to qualify for bank loans. This comprises the majority of today's entrepreneurs and business owners on the continent.
3. **Buyer:** In this example, it is Hyatt Regency in Addis-Ababa.
4. **Local Bank in this case, Awash Bank**: The role of the bank to guarantee the transaction.

John Doe has delivered the $1,000 worth of eggs to "*Hyatt Regency Hotel*" and is waiting for around 30 to 60 days to be paid. One of the major issues of small business owners is access to capital for day to day running and expansion. This transaction will be visible to all members of the platform as outlined above. Instead of John Doe waiting for up to 60 days for the $1,000, he now has an option to get $900 from a Diaspora investor within 24 to 48 hours for 10%. This does allow John Doe to quickly access capital to prepare (purchase feed, medicine, and other infrastructure needed to produce the set of eggs for delivery well under the normal time). This means that by the time the 60 days come around, John Doe would have already possibly been ready for his second supply instead of only just receiving his money to start the process again.

The Diaspora having bought this debt will instead be the one to be paid the $1,000 by the Hyatt Regency in 60 days. There are very few (if any) investments that would pay you 10% in 60 days today. Conversely, the $1,000 range is where the majority of African Diaspora fall. The role of Awash Bank is simply an insurance one. Awash Bank will take 2% of the transaction from the Diaspora. This assures the Diaspora that if Hyatt Regency does not pay in 60-days, Awash Bank will remit those funds to the Diaspora and legally pursue the funds from *"Hyatt Regency Hotel"*. This simple tool has brought more Diaspora into the investment space of their countries of origin. Small business owners have also found a low-risk source of capital that banks would not consider and at a lower rate than the going interest rates for African Banks today. This is a win-win investment mindset and at a scale that African Diaspora in partnership with local entities should be explored.

A similar thought process can be applied to purchasing orders. *Purchase Orders* (POs) are documents sent from you, as the buyer, to a supplier with a request for products or services as an order. Each PO will include a number for tracking the purchase order throughout the system, as well as the type of item, quantity, and agreed upon price. Given that the PO represents a promise and not a transaction that has already taken place, it implies higher risk. To this end, the investment in PO's will have a higher return (30% to 40%).

## The Africa Brain Gain:

There are more Ethiopian doctors in Chicago than in the whole of Ethiopia. Since the year 2000, 33 out of 85 American Nobel prize winners (in either physics, chemistry, or medicine),have been immigrants. The African diaspora has been winning Nobel prizes since Albert Camus in 1957 to Claude Simon in 1985 and Claude Cohen-Tannoudji (Physics in 1997). Examples of Diaspora contributions in their countries of residence are replete. Some common ones include the son of Abdul Fattah Jandali (a Syrian refugee), and Steve Jobs who revolutionized the computer world. Valued at $115 billion, this son of a Cuban immigrant (Jeff Bezos) is the richest man in the world. Even more fascinating is the fact that 43% of the fortune 500 companies today were either founded by immigrants or their children. This trend dates as far back as the founding of 1875 when today's largest telecom company (AT&T) was founded by a Scottish immigrant (Alexander Graham Bell). In 1994, a British immigrant Nigel

Morris started Capital One. Sergey Brin the co-founder of Google is a Russian immigrant. Elon Musk is perhaps the most famous African Diaspora. This son of Pretoria, South African Elon Musk is better known as the Tesla founder and is also the founder of PayPal, Space X, and many other highly innovative companies. Philip Emeagwali, a son of Akure Nigerian, won the Gordon Bell Prize (considered as the Nobel Prize of computing) for his contribution to the internet. The Algerian born Yves Saint Laurent became one of the world's biggest fashion icons. Teresa Heinz, heir to the Heinz ketchup fortune is a daughter of Maputo Mozamboque.

Over the years, the Diaspora have contributed to every aspect of their countries of residency. With a few exceptions such as Israel, many countries have struggled to attract their Diaspora and to also use them as conduits for the transfer of knowledge. In July of 1950, Israel passed the *"Law of Return"*. This law gives Jews the right to return and gain Israeli citizenship. In 1970 the same privileges were extended to people with one Jewish grandparent and a person who is married to a Jew.

In the coming Senegalese parliament, 10% of the parliamentarians will be members of the Diaspora. Most Diasporas do return home upon retirement and almost always demand to be buried at home. Additionally, most of the family members of the Diaspora are in their country of origin. This makes their input in national matters and participation in local politics equally paramount.

## Senegalese to Vote for 'Expat MPs':

Senegal MPs votes are to allow expatriates to run for office, expanding the size of the national assembly. Most African governments have sat back waiting for Diaspora to make a case because the top entrepreneurs, scientists, and dons in developing should be allowed to continue being part of the fabric of their country of origin. It is time these governments wake up and proactively incentivize these talented individuals to return. African governments should set aside a budget to lure Diaspora back home or at least to maintain ties. To set aside a fund under the ministry of foreign affairs that would facilitate expert diaspora's visits. Kwatsi Alibaruho (Ugandan) is a flight director at the National Aeronautics and Space Administration (NASA). He is the first black flight director at NASA. Uganda should have a program that pays for his annual vacation to Uganda, along with a minimum stipend. In exchange, Kwatsi will dedicate time during his visit to lecture at Makerere and carry out various workshops and consultations. The same can be applied to Bisi Ezerioha, an engineer and former pharmaceutical executive who has built some of the world's most powerful Honda and Porsche engines. The list is endless. It is similar initiatives that will strengthen the bond between the Diaspora and their countries of origin.

It is essential to the development of the continent to stress the strength of the Diaspora. Technology and infrastructure have made the globe virtually borderless. Today if America sneezes, Tanzania might catch a cold. African governments can no longer focus on geographical distance in the case of the Diaspora, while losing sight of the forest for the trees. There is not a better partner for economic and technological development today for Africa than its Diaspora. It is time to cut ties with old mindsets and wholeheartedly embrace her sons and daughters and work together as partners. However fixed the African government's mindset may seem, the tide of time and events will bring surprising positive changes in the relations between nations and their Diaspora. It is inevitable and time for Africa to unleash its developmental secret weapon, its Diaspora.

*********************************

# Lesson 11

## AFRICA MUST INNOVATE HER WAY OUT OF POVERTY - FOURTH INDUSTRIAL REVOLUTION AND AFRICA'S OPPORTUNITY TO CLOSE THE ECONOMIC GAP

**Industrial Revolution:**

The first industrial revolution dates back to the 1700s. This saw the transformation of agricultural societies into industrialized and urban ones. Thomas Newcomen's design of the steam train changed everything. It allowed the free movement of goods and labor. Goods that had once been crafted by hand started to be produced in mass quantities by machines in factories. The introduction of new machines, techniques in textiles, iron making, and other industries are helpful.

The Second Industrial Revolution was marked by rapid industrialization and standardization. This took place between 1870 and 1914 and came with the expansion of the electronics, steel, and textile industries. These advancements enabled the widespread of technologies such as the telegraph, railroad networks, water supply, sewage systems, and all. It was the telegraph and railroad lines that started the mass movement of ideas and started to lead people to the first signs of globalization, a prelude to today's society.

We are presently in the ending phase of the third industrial revolution, better known as the digital revolution. This has seen the advent of supercomputers and rapid advancements in the internet that has further redefined how people and businesses transact. People are standing on the palisade of the fourth industrial revolution. Unlike the previous iterations, this revolution seeks to marry physical, digital, and biological spheres to foster an inclusive, human-centered future. Another stark difference with the former revolutions is the deep-rooted desire to leverage technology to achieve the greatest good for the greatest number of people possible.

Moving forward, many people are expecting to see more prevalent use of technologies such as 3-D printing. This phenomenon has brought down the costs of labor and material. Fifth-generation wireless technology (5G) that is capable of reaching 100Gbps is focused on increasing bandwidth to be smarter and faster than ever before.

It is this technology that will power self-driving cars and the internet of things (IoT).

- **Self-Driving Cars**

Since May of 2019 UPS has been using self-driving trucks to ship goods between Phoenix and Tucson, Arizona. Recently '*Land O' Lakes*' announced that they delivered butter from Tulare, California, to Pennsylvania (almost 2,700miles) using self-driving trucks. These self-driving vehicles are designed to optimize traffic and fuel. It is being reported that 1.24 million people die each year from traffic collisions and this number is expected to reach 2.2 million in 2030 according to *'World Health Organization'* (WHO). According to a study by the Eno Centre for Transportation, if about 90% of cars on American roads were autonomous, the number of accidents would fall from six million a year to 1.3 million and deaths would fall from 33,000 to 11,300.

- ## Internet of Things (IoT)

Internet of Things (IoT) devices are taking human interaction out of the equation. Consumers are using the IoT to make restaurant reservations, monitor their exercise progress and overall health, as well as receive coupons for a store only by walking next to the business in question. Take an example in agriculture, devices using IoT technology can sense soil moisture and nutrients, in conjunction with weather data, better control smart irrigation and fertilizer systems. If the sprinkler systems dispense water only when needed, for example, this prevents wasting a precious resource. In manufacturing, RFID and GPS technology can help a manufacturer track a product from its start on the factory floor to its placement in the destination store; the whole supply chain from start to finish. These sensors can gather information on travel time, product condition, and environmental conditions that the product was subjected to. According to a Cisco report, the next decade will see IoT devices creating $14.4 trillion worth of value across several industries.

## The Ghana and South Korea Development Disparities:

In 1957, Ghana was the richest nation in sub-Saharan Africa with a per capita income of $490. That was nearly the same as South Korea which had a per capita income of $491. By the early 1980s, Ghana's per capita income had been reduced to $400 while South Korea's per capita income had grown to a whopping $2,000. By 1990 South Korea's per capita income was ten times larger than Ghana's ($4,832 versus $481). Today South Korea's GDP per capita stands at $26,761 while that of Ghana is $1,807.

South Korea, like many other Asian countries, embraced innovation and creativity. The first step was to revolutionize the education standard. With this, the illiteracy rate was falling from 80% to less than 10%. Towards the end of the 1980s, 37% of South Korean students had some form of higher education. South Korea notched top scores worldwide for manufacturing value-added as well as for tertiary efficiency - a measure that includes enrollment in higher education and the concentration of science and engineering graduates, said a recent '*Bloomberg*' report. Companies such as Samsung and LG have become global leaders in the area of consumer electronics due to their cutting-edge technology and innovative product designs.

Coupling with education, innovation and technology are the key factors that have underpinned South Korea's export competitiveness and fueled the country's remarkable economic rise over the past decades. The growth rate has been so impressive that the East Asian nation went from being one of the poorest countries in the 1960s to becoming the world's 12th largest economy in 2019, according to the World Bank. South Korea's $1.63T economy is bigger than Saudi Arabia and Turkey combined. America's global competitiveness is hinged on its innovative capacity and atmosphere. Digital technologies have been the vital factors of national security and economic growth. Additionally, these technologies are at the root of many advancements in complex sciences, healthcare, communications, and industry to mention a few.

There is a clear correlation between GDP growth and investment in innovation, research, and development. In the 15 years between 2000 and 2015, the US expenditure on research and development almost doubled from $268.6 billion to $496.6 billion. In the same period, the US GDP grew from $10.28T to $18.12 trillion. At the same time, India's investment almost tripled while China's increased tenfold and the results are similar.

Besides, technological advances are helping to bring down the cost of renewable energies, such as solar and wind energy, handing them a greater role in the global economy's energy mix, with significant effects for both producers and consumers of fossil fuels. A simple example of the benefits, in the developing countries a slight reduction to the cost of gas at the pump brought about by technology, can mean a lowered cost of transportation which means a lower cost of food, cement, and clothing just to mention a few. This also means additional savings at the pump allowing one to save more and invest in stocks. A new McKinsey Global Institute report, beyond the super-cycle, technology is reshaping resources, speaks to how technology can aid in the further unlocking of $900B to $1.6T in savings globally by 2035. This is more than the GDP of Spain.

## What Can Africa Learn from South Korea?

Most African countries, with a few exceptions like Rwanda, have decided to first become rich and then focus on people. This is the exact opposite of what nations like Korea did and in line with what Rwanda's Kagame is doing with Presidential Scholars and other programs. So, investing in people is the more ideal route to pursue.

South Korea is intent on joining the globe's top 4 nations in artificial intelligence (AI) and has invested $2B in programs to ensure this vision is realized by 2022. Some of the key initiatives include 6 new AI institutions that seek to churn out more than 5,000 engineers.

Like South Korea, Africa has to look inwards and seek homegrown solutions that work for them. South Korea resides in the same region as China and Japan. China has low labor costs. Japan was leading the way with high-tech and capital-intensive industries. Today's 10 youngest populations are all in Africa. Average ages include Niger (14.8 years), Uganda (15.9 years), and Zambia (16.9 years). By 2034 Africa will have the youngest working-age population. Additionally, "*Times Magazine*" has estimated Africa's urbanization rate to be at 37%. This is more than India's and on par with China and it is expected to be the fastest between 2020 and 2050.

South Korea invested in building a national consensus with regards to the direction of the major economic policies. Concurrently, there was a high level of government support of the local entrepreneurs that helped them optimize the business opportunities available. Above all, the key miracle of South Korea has been in the mindset of the population that allows them to successfully adapt to challenges while minimizing risks.

## The Way Forward:

An IMF report released in April 2017 confirmed that oil-exporting countries and other resource-intensive countries in Sub-Saharan Africa were showing the worst economic performance in the region. Even those that enjoyed good governance were also experiencing similar challenges. For a long time, continents have relied on agricultural produce that remains vulnerable due to the instability of international market prices.

Even a country like Botswana that enjoyed a reputation for good governance and was regarded as a model in Sub-Saharan Africa, experienced problems related to a commodity-dependent economy. Traditionally, African economies that are primarily reliant on agricultural produce like cacao, coffee, and tea have experienced vulnerability with the fluctuation of international market prices. While commodity prices have been recovering in

2018, various economic forecasts point to rather sluggish growth for the resource-rich African countries.

The African Union has come up with an agenda for 2063 that is intended to inspire nations to achieve a structurally transformed economy. This primarily leans on an industrialized Africa. It is evident that without proper investment in human capital development and more in innovation and technology, this dream will never be realized.

Stephen Hawking once famously said, *"Intelligence is the ability to adapt to change."* A decade ago, terms such as the internet of things, machine learning, and artificial intelligence were not common phrases. Today, most labor-intensive tasks have been taken away from humans and are being dealt with purely by machines. The world is changing at such a high pace that in a few decades most of these novel technologies will also be obsolete. The only way to keep up is with heavy investment in human capital and constant investment in research and development. The labor force must be retrained, upskilled, and transformed.

One way to achieve this would be strategic partnership between academia and the private sector to allow the effective transfer of knowledge. This allows university students to constantly keep up with evolving trends of the real world. Curriculums will also need to be constantly updated to this effect. The McKinsey Global Institute's report posited that *"Artificial Intelligence"* (AI) alone has the potential to add up to $13trillion to the current global GDP by 2030. The automation of labor alone is said to contribute around $9trillion and innovation in products and services could increase by $6trillion.

The renowned American economist Robert Shiller once said *"you cannot wait until a house burns down to buy fire insurance on it. We cannot wait until there are massive dislocations in our society to prepare for the Fourth Industrial Revolution"*. Indeed, the time for Africa to prepare herself for the fourth industrial revolution is yesterday. African governments must also encourage experimentation. Like venture capitalists do with their investment, African governments should also take a portfolio approach to scripting policies. This way success balances failure and models that work can be scaled up. A November 2019 World Bank article has shown how the Ethiopian government is developing a *"Portfolio"* of industrial parks as a means of making Ethiopia the continent's manufacturing hub. The Liberian government experiment with outsourcing school management to private sector entities. A recent report from poverty action has shown that this has yielded positive results. After 3 years of this experiment, these schools raised their test scores by 0.21standard deviations in math and 0.16 standard deviations in English.

## Drive Mass Personalization of Products and Services:

Africa must shift focus to creating more adaptive governments. The African private sector should be the driver of the innovative change while the government remains the enabler through creative and adaptive governments as well as an appropriate allocation of resources. Business leaders and entrepreneurs should remain focused on a few key consumer behaviors. They should focus on creating maximum value from a single transaction by using Artificial Intelligence (AI) and other technologies to best predict future needs and points of engagement. There should be an unwavering emphasis on collaboration with multiple partners beyond one's supply chain network. Companies must embrace risk to foster growth as well as providing the best value for the customers. Only in doing so will these companies keep up with or stay ahead of the competition.

*********************************

# Lesson 12

## THE UNBREAKABLE CHAIN: BLOCKCHAIN AND THE HEALTHCARE SYSTEM

### What is Blockchain?

As the name suggests fundamentally, blockchain is just a chain of blocks. However, in this case, the block is simply digital information stored in a public database (the chain). It is the stringing of the blocks together that forms a blockchain.

These are made up of three parts of digital information.

- The blocks store information about a transaction, such as a date and time.

- Secondly, the block stores information about the participant in the transaction.

- Thirdly, blocks store a unique identifier called a hash.

When a new block is added to the blockchain, it is quickly added for anyone to view. To look at the Bitcoin blockchain it will have complete visibility into the transaction data, along with pertinent information like what time it was added, where it was added, and by who. One can connect their computer to the blockchain network and get automatic updates when any change is made. In today's world, the most common example is the Facebook news feed when someone posts new updates.

## Is Blockchain as secure as they say?

To start with, every block is added linearly and chronologically. Each block in Bitcoin blockchain has a position on the chain which is called a height. The Bitcoin height is 608,434 and each block contains its hash and that of the block before it.

Hash codes are created by a mathematical function that turns digital information into a string of numbers and letters. If that information is edited in any way, the hash code changes as well. Since the blocks are connected, the next block will have the old hash. To get away with this in the case of Bitcoin, it needs to update over 608,000 blocks of hash. So, recalculating all these hashes will need improbable computing power which makes it hard to edit and impossible to delete.

## Healthcare and Blockchain Technology:

Blockchain healthcare use cases are being discovered by the day, and with them, the entire healthcare system can be completely fixed. Many healthcare and blockchain companies are currently working on or have already released blockchain-based systems to improve healthcare for both professionals and patients. The recording technology facilitates the secure transfer of patient medical records and manages the medicine supply chain. In healthcare, medication, clinical supplies, blood products, and medical devices are examples. Where blockchain is being used for operations, compliance, and forecasting among pharmaceutical manufacturers, blood banks providers, and pharmacies.

Enlisting and retentively remain two of the major challenges in clinical trials, and despite countless attempts over the years, enhancement remains largely unrealized. Clinical trial data sharing and the skill for research participants to experience value discovery are some of the promises of blockchain for these use cases.

One of the most popular healthcare use cases for blockchain is patient data management. Medical records tend to be separated by health agencies, making it impossible to determine a patient's medical history without consulting their previous care provider. This process can take a significant amount of time and may often result in mistakes due to human error. This system selects patient agency, giving a transparent and accessible view of medical history. It is planning to store all of a patient's information in one place, making it easier for patients and doctors to view. Blockchain maintains the reliability of health records while establishing a single point of truth. Doctors, hospitals, and laboratories can all request patient information that has a record of origin and protects the patient's identity from outside sources.

Artificial Intelligence and blockchain also offer patients a single point of care. The company organizes wearable diagnostic tools and telemedicine sessions to gather patient information and share it with the patient's medical team. Doctors use the blockchain to securely gather patient information and share it with a patient's healthcare providers. Blockchain is a platform in medical care that facilitates the searching, sharing, storage, buying, and selling of genetic information. The company protects its users' privacy by allowing only other members to purchase genetic information using safe, traceable DNA tokens. Member companies can use genetic information to build upon their genetic knowledge and advance the industry.

Blockchain would also help tag and track drugs at every stage of the supply chain. It will act as a medium to assure the authenticity of the drugs. Patients will also have control over the data stored in the blockchain. Others can view their data only if the patients grant them permission. Blockchain is an exciting development that promises to change the way people live. This piece of technology is undergoing further progress and will continue to a growing list of potential use cases.

## Other Use Cases:

In 2018 the African country of Sierra Leon carried the world's first blockchain-supported elections. In 2018 *Overstock's Medici* partnered with the government of *"Rwanda's Land Management and Use Authority and Information Society"* to develop blockchain-based land management and property rights platform (A.P). *Moller-Maersk* partnered with *IBM* to develop the *"Trade Lens Supply Chain Platform"* using blockchain to track cargo ships and containers.

\*\*\*\*\*\*\*\*\*\*\*\*\*\*\*\*\*\*\*\*\*\*\*\*\*\*\*\*\*\*\*\*\*\*\*\*\*\*

# Lesson 13

## DEMAND & SUPPLY PLANNING: SOLVING THE FOOD SECURITY CHALLENGE

### Introduction:

Demand Planning is all about managing and planning for customer demand. Supply Planning is about managing and planning the inventory supply to meet customer demand. Another definition of demand and supply planning is the process of forecasting the demand for a product or service so it can be produced and delivered more efficiently to the satisfaction of the customers. Demand planning is considered an essential step in supply chain planning. Supply planning is the component of supply chain management involved with determining how to best fulfill the requirements created from the demand plan. The objective is to balance supply and demand in a manner that achieves the financial and service objectives of the enterprise.

### Demand Planning:

Assessing future demand is one of the most appreciated activities an organization can undertake. A demand plan's impact is felt throughout the business, from sales and marketing to manufacturing and distribution. When done correctly, demand planning can put a person in an outstanding position to deliver outstanding customer service while meeting his/her business goals.

People who are responsible for demand planning gather information from the sales and marketing, operations, and finance sections to estimate how much of a company's products that customers will want to buy at various points in the future. Better-quality demand planning provides countless benefits including lower costs of inventory, reduced waste, and an increase in on-time, in-full deliveries, reduction in advanced shipping fees. Poor demand planning can also create too much inventory, which can lead to waste, less obvious costs, lost credibility, and wasted resources.

## Supply Planning:

It is the part of supply chain management involved with determining how to best fulfill the requirements created from the demand plan. The objective is to balance supply and demand in a manner that achieves the financial and service objectives of the enterprise. A supply plan is another component of the *"Sales and Operations Planning (S&OP)"* process. Supply planning comes after demand planning. Supply planning includes demand prioritization, procurement, capacity planning, supplier management, order scheduling, and stockyard planning. Hence different kinds of decisions are made during supply planning, while it also reduces the variability in production.

The efficiency of such planning involves the accuracy of data. The supply planning process begins with an approved demand plan. If a person is using a supply chain planning software system, such as "*Demand Caster*", the demand translation step will automatically allocate the demand plan to the location where the demand for a specific customer is typically fulfilled. An automated software system should then use the customer order record to identify the ship-from location and then generate a forecast to be applied against a specific ship-from location.

## Food and Agriculture Organization (FAO):

In 1945 the '*Food and Agriculture Organization (FAO)*' was founded to reduce food losses and wastage. However, as of last year, it is estimated that more than 30% of the produced food is not consumed. The "*World Bank*" estimates that for every 1% reduction in post-harvest loss, there is a $40M in output gain that primarily goes back to the farmers. Some reports have estimated wasted food each year to be an amount that can feed 1.6 billion people. The total cost of wasted food is approximately $1 trillion. The underlying issue is a post-harvest loss. An alarming fact is that by 2050 the world population is expected to be 9 billion people. Africa will contribute to half of that increase. The only way these people will be fed is if food production is increased by about 70%.

More troubling is the fact that the production resources needed such as land and water are inelastic. This means that the only simple solution is cutting down the post-harvest loss to ensure a higher percentage of the food produced reaches the population. This can only be achieved by accurate demand, supply prediction, and planning. With such, it can better collaborate with the various stages of the supply chain and can also reduce the cumulative effects of the agriculture markets causing shortages and crises.

## How accurate is the forecasting?

The Random Forest (RF) model has been used to predict sugarcane yield based on simulated biomass indices, observed climate, and seasonal climate prediction indices. The forecasting accuracy reached 95.45%. Not all models are as accurate and a lot of advancements in the application of big data have tremendously increased the accuracy of these models. Some key factors used in this prediction include climate, demand for the crop products, government policy, level of adoption of new technologies, crop cycle, promotion, price, and the seed.

*********************************

# Lesson 14

## THE NEW REALITIES: AR & VR

**Augmented Reality and Virtual Reality:**

Augmented Reality and Virtual Reality are two of the ways that can change the way people look at the world. Often, people think AR and VR are similar things. Augmented Reality and Virtual Reality are increasingly used in technology, so the difference is important. Augmented Reality and Virtual Reality are the opposite of one another with what each technology seeks to accomplish and deliver for the user. Virtual Reality offers a digital regeneration of a real-life setting, while Augmented Reality delivers virtual elements as an overlay to the real world.

In other words, Augmented Reality is an enhanced version of reality created by the use of technology to add digital information to an image of something. Whereas Virtual Reality is the use of computer technology to create a simulated environment. Unlike traditional user interfaces, VR places the user inside an experience. Instead of viewing a screen in front of them, users are immersed and able to interact with 3D worlds. By simulating as many senses as possible, such as vision, hearing, touch, and even smell, the computer is transformed into a gatekeeper to this artificial world. The only limits to near-real VR experiences are the availability of content and cheap computing power.

## Some Use Cases of Augmented Reality:

From interior design to architecture and construction, *"Augmented Reality"* is helping professionals to imagine their final products during the creative process. The use of headsets enables architects, engineers, and design professionals to step directly into their buildings. It allows them to see how their designs might look, and even make virtual on-the-spot changes. Augmented Reality also helps in the medical field. AR can make digital images and provide critical information available to surgeons in 3D and within their field of view. Surgeons will not need to look away from the surgical field to access crucial information they might require to perform a successful procedure.

Technology such as tablets have become extensive in many schools and classrooms, teachers are now ramping up student's learning experience with Augmented Reality. The Aurasma app is already being used in classrooms so that students can view their classes via a smartphone or tablet for a richer learning environment.

## Some Use Cases of Virtual Reality:

Virtual Reality enables businesses to promote products in a completely new way. VR experiences are a natural allowance to the video gaming industry. But as VR becomes more mainstream, gaming companies can increase their markets by introducing products to new audiences. With specialized accessories, VR-enabled games will not require mastering of complicated and sometimes confusing controllers.

There are already many companies using Virtual Reality for employee training. For instance, Walmart is currently using *"Oculus Go"* headsets to help onboard new employees by teaching them about new technology, compliance, and customer service skills. VR can simulate real-life experiences, which is invaluable when it comes to employee training.

## What Next:

Next-generation education will be completely transformed by AR/VR. This technology will empower students with holistic learning that adds on social, emotional, and creative components through intuitive experiences and simulations.

It is estimated that by 2023 there will be a tremendous increase of AR devices from about 900 million today to almost 2.5 billion. *"Market Watch"* estimates the industry in total will cross the $117B mark by 2024 US *"Farmers Insurance"* is presently working on a program to help workers improve their interpersonal skills using VR that uses Artificial Intelligence powered by a virtual human. AT&T is planning on utilizing its 5G technology to resolve medical challenges. In partnership with VITAS, AT&T intends to use AR/VR enabled devices to reduce pain and anxiety for terminally ill patients in hospice by providing calming or distracting content.

\*\*\*\*\*\*\*\*\*\*\*\*\*\*\*\*\*\*\*\*\*\*\*\*\*\*\*\*\*\*\*\*\*\*\*\*

# Lesson 15

## MACHINE LEARNING - TURNING CURRENT CHALLENGES TO NEW OPPORTUNITIES

### Introduction:

Machine learning is an application of Artificial Intelligence (AI) that provides systems with the ability to automatically learn and improve from experience without being programmed. Machine learning focuses on the development of computer programs that can access data and use it to learn for themselves. Another definition of it is *"Machine Learning is a set of rules that a computer develops on its own to correctly solve difficulties. The basic idea is that a Machine Learning computer will find outlines in data and then predict the outcome of something it has never seen before."* The intelligent systems built on machine learning algorithms can learn from experience or historical data.

Machine learning algorithms can process more information and spot more configurations than their human counterparts. One study was used (CAD) to review the early mammography scans of women who later recognized breast cancer, and the computer spotted 50% of the cancers as much as a year before the women were formally diagnosed. Moreover, machine learning can be used to understand disease in large populations.

## Benefits of Machine Learning:

Machine learning is verifying that it can be a benefit to help to remove false alarms and spot things that human screeners might miss in security screenings at airports, stadiums, malls, clinics, bus stations, and other places which can speed up the process and guarantee safer events. For industries that include monetary transactions, detecting fraud is difficult. Since digital transactions have greatly increased in recent years, the risk of fraud has too. With machine learning, businesses can review millions of transactions and identify doubtful activity faster than with human experts.

Machine learning in the form of artificial intelligence can be used to grade student projects and exams more accurately than a human can. It may require some input from a human being, but the results will have higher validity and trustworthiness. Machine learning in the form of artificial intelligence also has the potential to make educators better organized by completing tasks such as classroom management, scheduling, etc. In turn, teachers are free to focus on tasks that cannot be achieved by Artificial Intelligence, and that require a human touch.

Search engines depending on Machine Learning to improve their services is no secret today. Applying these, Google has introduced some amazing services. For example, voice recognition, image search, and many more. Using Machine Learning, a person can synthesize the information in data and make appropriate conclusions, such as a person's interests.

According to Reg Chua, COO of Reuters News, technologies are close to providing customized news, market reports, and newsrooms are starting to embrace the possibilities. Soon people will start to receive customized news and financial reports on demand. These reports will not be generic but ones that will be able to compare the investment portfolio and its performance against the broader market with explanation, to boot. For example, it is 2:13 PM and the market is 4.2% up but the portfolio is 1.5% down. This is owed in part to the purchase of stock "X" which is purchased 10 days ago and has since fallen sharply due to.

Shortly, it is expected that robots will become more intelligent at performing various tasks. Robots, drones in assembling places, and different sorts of robots are potentially going to be used progressively to make our lives easier. Machine learning is one of the most troublesome innovations of this 21st era. Even though this innovation can even now be considered as a beginning, its future is impressive.

************************************

# Lesson 16

## INTERNET OF THINGS (IOT)

*"Today and Tomorrow"*

IoT is simply the network of interconnected things/devices which are embedded with sensors, software, network connectivity, and necessary electronics that enable them to collect and exchange data, making them responsive. In other words, the internet of things is a system of interrelated computing devices, mechanical and digital machines, objects, animals, or people that are provided with *"Unique Identifiers"* (UIDs). It is the ability to transfer data over a network without requiring human-to-human or human-to-computer interaction. The *"Internet of Things"* is a pretty simple theory that means taking all the useful things in the world and connecting them to the internet.

### Applications of (Internet of Things):

IoT applications are expected to prepare billions of everyday objects with connectivity and intelligence. It is already being organized extensively in various domains. Wearable technology is a mark of IoT applications and is one of the earliest industries to have deployed the IoT at its service. Today the use of *"Fit Bits"*, heart rate monitors, and smartwatches are everywhere. Like the example of Jarvis, which is an AI system that Zuckerberg has built to control his home and perform basic tasks, such as turning the lights off or on, control a particular room's temperature, playing music, opening doors, and so on.

Livestock monitoring is about animal farming and cost-saving. People use IoT applications to gather data about the health and well-being of cattle, breeders. By using IoT, people get to know earlier about the sick animal and help avoid a great number of sick cattle.

IoT provides a chance for retailers to connect with customers to increase the in-store experience. Imagine walking into a fitting room at TJ Max equipped with sensors and an interactive screen. The sensors can communicate the items that are being tried on with the interactive screen. In turn, the screen displays other complimentary items also sold in the store. Smartphones will be the way for retailers to remain connected with their customers even out of the store.

Farmers are using meaningful visions from the data to yield a better return on investment. Sensing for soil moisture and nutrients, controlling water usage for plant growth, and determining custom fertilizer are some simple uses of IoT.

## The Future of IoT:

By 2024, it is estimated that there will be more than $20 billion IoT devices. In 2013, there were more than 4.3 billion things connected to the internet, according to IoT analytics. By 2019 the market will increase to nearly 11.3 billion IoT devices. The future of IoT has a huge possibility of unfolding in the automotive industry. 50 % of US drivers do not feel safe sharing the road with driverless cars. Moreover, 72% of Americans are afraid of riding in a self-driving car but these circumstances are unfolded. Since the competition is more than just high, and according to Forbes, apart from the main market players, over 1700 startups are entering the competition, it will not be long until bots are driving our smart cars.

*********************************

# Lesson 17

## ROLE OF BIG DATA IN TODAY'S BUSINESS ENVIRONMENT

In today's data-driven environment, businesses utilize and make big profits from big data. Big data, in turn, empowers businesses to make decisions based on trends, facts, and statistical numbers. Also, in the digital era, with so much information out there, business leaders need the right kind of software for sifting through the noise and catching hold of the right information. This is required to make the best decisions, great strategies, and allow rapid growth.

**Importance of Data in Business:**

Nearly every business decision that is made has data at its core.

- Online resources offer a lot of information to the human resource directors so that they can confirm details and determine the best candidate to recruit.

- Market segmentation data has proven to be a boon to marketing departments which can now speed up the sale-closing process whenever possible, as such data helps them find customers who are ready to buy.

- Business executives examine bigger trends in the market, like fluctuations and changes in the pricing of resources, their manufacturing, shipping, etc.

- Effective utilization of data can help companies streamline the process of development of their product and finally deliver it to the customers.

- Big data can also monitor the finances by saving the costs of shotgun advertising or higher pay for a resource. This can significantly improve the company's profits.

In other words, big data can be transformed into business strategies for targeting the right audience and enhancing profits.

**Business Applications of Big Data:**

From front-facing customer interactions to internal insights, big data can present an abundance of new growth opportunities.

Three of the major ones include automation, in-depth insights, and better decision making:

- **Automation**

Through robotic process automation, big data has the potential to improve operations and internal efficiencies. Canonical chunks of real time-data can be built into business processes through careful analysis of automated decision making. Automating data collection and storage is within reach, so people can have decreasing cloud computing costs and scalable IT infrastructure.

- **In-Depth Insights**

By reviewing large sets of data, hidden opportunities can be discovered now, which were unknown to organizations before. These complex data sets can be used to enhance existing products and develop new ones. The competitive landscape that people have in today's era, makes proprietary data within the market invaluable.

- **Faster, Better Decision Making**

Businesses are now able to analyze information instantly and make smart, informed decisions due to the speed of data analytics technology, paired with the ability to analyze new sources of data.

## How to Harness the Power of Big Data?

With over 40% of large organizations investing in big data since 2012, the market for big data is skyrocketing. However, it can be overwhelming for someone wanting to begin on this path, due to the endless possible data points which demand management.

Consider the following points before choosing and implementing a big data solution:

- ## The Experienced BigData Team

Team members should be able to manipulate big data sets, understand modern analytic methods, and include experienced consultants who understand overarching business goals.

- ## Identify End Goals

To successfully implement a big data solution, the first step is to have the right set of objectives. The data analytics must be properly aligned with the organization's end goals, whether it be brand recognition, greater profit, or market share.

- ## Capture the Right Data

The backbone of the entire big data process is the next step, which is to identify, capture, and track the right data.

- ## Apply Proper Analytic Methods

To make quick business decisions, the supporting team needs to have easily digestible data and their visual summaries.

## Make the Best Use of Big Data Today:

The right use and application of big data provide a competitive edge over the business counterparts. A company that has a dedicated team working on big data can easily gain hidden insights from the client's interactions, something that their competitors do not have access to.

\*\*\*\*\*\*\*\*\*\*\*\*\*\*\*\*\*\*\*\*\*\*\*\*\*\*\*\*\*\*\*\*\*\*\*\*

# Lesson 18

## ARTIFICIAL INTELLIGENCE AND COUNSELLING

A large population of individuals struggles with mental health and yet few receive the required treatment. Suicide rates are high and there are many that attempt. The ramifications of mental health being untreated has a huge impact on families, cultures, and the economy with the cost of treatment and loss of productivity. There is a shortage of mental health professions with many people living remotely or unable to afford or connect with the required professional help.

Many individuals use technology to help them in every area of their life. People have Siri on their phones, Lexa, and Google to help them with directions, music, and reminders. Many of them turn to Google when they are not feeling well, diagnosing themselves with WebMD or simply looking for advice with regards to their relationships, nutrition, fitness, general, health, and wellness. There is also the development of specific apps that will support people with their mental health. Mental health apps offer great support for people who may not be able to access traditional therapy. Mental health apps are also a great addition to traditional therapy. Many of the apps are free or require a small fee and they are programmed with several therapeutic techniques from stress reduction to "*Cognitive Behavioral Therapy*", and address everything from anxiety, depression to eating disorders, bipolar, trauma, obsessive-compulsive disorder, and more.

AI is offering many benefits to the mental health field. People can access AI 24/7 where individuals do not have to wait to book an appointment when they are in a crisis or need support. AI is also offering professional health support as Algorithms can analyze data much quicker than humans. AI is also able to monitor patients' progress, alert a professional when there are concerns, suggest possible treatment and support in its delivery. Many individuals have also admitted that they feel more comfortable talking to a bot over a person as they feel they will not be judged. Also, research has shown that through interacting with a robot, people begin to treat them as though they were real.

Psychologist, Dr. Alison Darcy created "*Woebot*", a Facebook-integrated computer program that reproduces conversations a therapist might have with a patient. Woebot is a chatbot that resembles an instant messaging service. It offers "*Cognitive Behavioral Therapy*" while asking about a person's mood, thoughts, and responses to how he/she is feeling. It can learn about a person and emulates a real face to face meeting. Chatbots are consistently improving and able to offer more human-like and natural support and interactions.

Ellie is another chatbot created by the Institute of "*Creative Technologies*" (ICT) that can detect not only words but also nonverbal cues (posture, facial expression, gestures). Non-verbal cues are very important in therapy and can be hard to detect.

Technology is expanding with IA at the forefront. There are mixed reviews with regards to this expansion in technology, with some fearing the takeover of machines and the possible loss of jobs. People are excited about the potential support that technology may offer them. For now though AI and other technological advances are supporting the mental health field. AI has yet to replace a good therapist but when combined can offer greater support that is affordable and able to reach more people.

*********************************

# Lesson 19

# EMOTIONAL RECOGNITION

## Some Information About Emotion Recognition:

Emotion Detection is a technique used to read the emotions on a human face by using hi-tech image processing software. The program can recognize emotions, such as anger, sadness, fear, joy, disgust, surprise, trust, and so on. The most common and spontaneous way to identify emotions is via facial detection in photos and videos. As Emotion recognition technology keeps improving and expanding, emotion recognition is used by different companies, banks, airports, and sports. For example, to allow call centers to be as responsive as possible to customers, software that identifies emotions is now in use. This software not only understands and analyzes the content of conversations but also detects the caller's mood. The accuracy of these systems is now in the range of 85-93 percent. For example, an angry customer can be detected from the beginning and can be routed to a well-trained agent who can also monitor in real-time how the conversation is going and adjust.

Many insurance companies are also using *"Emotion Recognition"* for identifying fraud. Insurance companies use voice analysis to detect whether a customer is telling the truth when submitting a claim. According to independent surveys, up to 30%

of users have admitted to lying to their car insurance company to gain coverage.

Many companies use *'Emotion Recognition'* in their interviews; some employ this technology to screen prospective candidates based on factors like body language and mood. In doing so, a company can find a person whose personality and characteristics are best suited to the job. In the *"Automatic Teller Machine"* (ATM) Emotion Recognition is also used. The ATM will not be dispensing money when people are feeling scared.

Partnerships between emotion AI technology vendors and surveillance camera providers have emerged. Cameras in public places in the *"United Arabic Emirates"* can detect people's facial expressions and understand the general mood of the population. Digital marketing professionals are leveraging the power of emotion detection to understand the emotions of their potential customers to improve customer experiences and to create a lasting bond. To begin with, analyzing various facial expressions and behavior can help figure out the emotional state of a customer. So, Emotion Recognition is improving people's lives in many ways.

\*\*\*\*\*\*\*\*\*\*\*\*\*\*\*\*\*\*\*\*\*\*\*\*\*\*\*\*\*\*\*\*\*\*\*

# Lesson 20

## Upstream Thinking

*"Solving Problems Caused by Innovation"*

**Upstream Thinking:**

Read about upstream thinking by the medical sociologist, Irving Zola. Zola speaks of a witness that sees a man caught in a river current. The witness saves the man, only to be drawn to the rescue of more drowning people. After many have been rescued, the witness walks upstream to investigate why so many people have fallen into the river. While Zola was thinking of public health and how innovators who are burdened with solving a present problem need to plan and innovate for the problems that will arise from these solutions.

Innovations are ideas or creative thoughts that have been transformed into practical reality in the form of a gadget or strategy by new imagination. In business, innovation helps them to grow and plays a very important role in terms of economic growth. It helps problem solve, especially as the world's problems continue to evolve. Innovation helps companies stay on top of constantly changing problems, especially in developing countries. People have many examples of companies resisted to innovate and inadvertently leading to their demise. These include Blockbuster, Kodak, Polaroid, Nokia, and Blackberry. Technology advancements have helped people with disabilities by giving them more autonomy. Innovations have made society more inclusive and communities more accessible.

## Technologies for the Rectifications of Social Problems:

Solar panels and wind turbines, the internet, computers, punched cards, optical scan voting, medical equipment, and voice recognition are the technologies invented for the rectification of major social problems such as climate change, poverty, education, the economy, voting, health care, and public safety.

The simplest way to categorize innovation is into four types:

- **Incremental innovation** is improvement in an existing thing such as products, processes, or services. For a business, this is a product, process, or business idea or combinations that have been enacted in the commercial center that produces new benefits and development for the association. Cadbury, for example, introduces new flavors to their product line to satisfy customer's needs. Incremental innovation consists of small, yet meaningful improvements in your products, services, and other ways in which a person does business.

- **Disruptive innovation** is when a company introduces a new consumer category. "*Netflix*" is a textbook example of successful disruptive innovation. Starting as a company supplying DVD mail-outs, Netflix offered a cost-effective and convenient product to an area of the market that was previously overlooked. Netflix disrupted "*Blockbuster's*" business by making their services more innovative and modernized, more accessible from anywhere, and gave personalized options to users that "*Blockbuster*" was never able to match.

- **Transformational innovation** is the introduction of technology that creates a new industry and transforms the way people live and work. The iPhone has become a ubiquitous accessory around the world and has changed the way to communicate, connect, create, and much more. What made the iPhone transformative was the shift in concept underpinning the entire iPhone project. Its designers did not create a telephone with some extra features, but rather a full-fledged hand-held computer that could also make calls and browse the internet. Apple continues to be a disruptor and pacesetter in the industry.

- **Radical innovation** is finding an entirely new way of doing something that it blows up the existing system or process and replaces it with something entirely new. When asked about his car invention Henry Ford said, "*If I had asked people what they wanted, they would have said faster horses.*" Few inventions have had as profound an impact on the world as the car. It was an invention that has not only changed the way people lived, but it has also influenced business and the economy in ways no one could have foreseen when Henry Ford put together a mass-production operation for his "*Model T*".

## Negative Impacts of Innovations:

## Human Interaction Fading Away:

The invention of the telegraph did make the world a lot smaller. It helps send information across the country faster than any vehicle. The electric telegraph was invented in 1837. It was the first device that could electronically send text-based messages from one location to another. The first telegram, sent by Samuel Morse (who invented the Morse Code), only traveled two miles. This simple innovation later helped the train station be more effective by knowing exactly when the trains would go to which station. This made the stations operate smoother and have more departures and less waiting time for the people boarding on to them. The progeny of the telegraph is the text message. Today, these text messages are used to ask for feedback, send parcel delivery notifications, carry out security authorizations, confirm appointments, and so much more. The business-to-consumer text messages are often called "*SMS Notifications*" and are usually sent to announce special events or in response to transactions. Texts have also squeezed out the human part in communication. Morse use to write very long letters and used wonderful prose that described everything around him. But today when people use texts, they do not have that luxury. Additionally, when humans communicate, they use a lot of different ways of getting a message across besides words. As a result of communicating in this one-dimensional way, what historians, linguists, and scholars are concerned with is that people are reducing the ability to empathize.

This useful technology has led to an addiction to smartphones, which is a major problem. This technology has led to a lot of wasted time, instead of actual use for research and studies due to countless apps for entertainment and access to all. Social Interaction has become limited. The excessive use of mobile phones has exposed the population to harmful radio-frequency fields emitted from mobile phones. A study by Columbia hospital shows that the constant and continued exposure in the past years has increased the risk of lesser-known skin problems. The radiations from the phone are electromagnetic rays in the microwave range (850–1800), much of which is received by the skin.

Excessive listening to music can cause hearing problems. They may cause headaches, decreased attention, shortness of temper, sleep disorders, and depression, mostly among teenagers. Students also have access to illegal watching of vulgarity which influences them negatively, inciting them for wrong. Cyber-crime is a new face of a crime that has emerged due to technology. More than a facility for quick search, smartphones have become boredom killing devices.

## Artificial Light & Insomnia:

Indubitably, where electricity is a major beneficial invention for humans along with artificial light, it also seems to harm our health. In the past, people had a healthy routine. Today, people are scheduled by too many things and majorly by clocks. Ainissa

Ramirez in her book *"The Alchemy of Us"* discussed the impacts of the invention of a clock in the first chapter '*Interact*' saying that sleep was in segments at first. These segments were called first and second sleep and everyone slept that way. The Tiv tribe in Nigeria still employs the terms *"first sleep"* and *"second sleep"* to refer to specific periods of the night.

Artificial light seems to be also impacting people's health because their bodies have two modes, a daytime mode, and a night-time mode. Night-time exposure to light, especially blue-spectrum light, can decrease the production and secretion of melatonin, depending on the intensity and wavelength of the light. The body knows which mode to be in based on blue light. Now, the ancestors lived by sunlight, which has a lot of blue in it, and candlelight which had less. But people live under artificial lights all the time. When they are in daytime mode, their bodies are in growth mode and that is impacting them because their cells will respond to that growth mode in ways that people do not necessarily want. A team led by the *"Barcelona Institute for Global Health (IS Global)"*, a center supported by the *"la Caixa Foundation"*, has conducted the first study of the association between night-time exposure to outdoor artificial light and colorectal cancer. The findings, published in *Epidemiology*, show that exposure to the blue light spectrum may increase the risk of this type of cancer. Insomnia was not this common among people in the past before the invention of clocks. The risk of heart attack is 11% higher on Mondays as compared to other days of the week, possibly due to sleep lost while readjusting to the schedule of the working week.

**An air conditioner** is the artificial cooling of the room if someone lives in a hot area but it also makes humanly addicted and thus the human body's moderate temperature is varied. Continuous usage of air conditioners affect health, making the human body sensitive to hot weather as there is repercussion when one has to face hot weather outside, the body bears it hardly and opt heat-related illness. More, sudden changes in temperature and humidity affect the respiratory system.

## Butterfly Effect Approach:

In an attempt to explain the complex mathematical chaos theory "Edward Lorenz, the meteorology professor at MIT came up with the butterfly effect. Lorenz meant that a small event such as a butterfly flapping its wings in the *"Amazon forest"* at the right time and place would trigger a set of events that will ultimately culminate in the formation of a tsunami in Kenya. Today, people have female oral contraceptives and hormone therapy drugs that cause blood clots. *"Tamoxifen (Nolvadex)"*, which is used to treat breast cancer and was found to increase the risk of uterine cancer. Antipsychotic treating drugs such as *"Zyprexa"* led to sudden cardiac death.

In the short term, people can employ simple solutions such as limiting the excessive use of technology. Others include the implementation of natural means of resolving some challenges.

There is a growing need for parents to monitor children and themselves about the use of technology. Instead, children can work on cognitive development instead of letting them dependent on technology. However, people must also think hard about the long-term implications of their innovation.

It is time for innovators to think upstream as they solve today's problems. People are presently equipped with powerful analytical tools that if properly utilized will avert the adverse side effects of innovation to human life and ultimately the environment people live in. Policies should be in place showing concerted efforts that are made to account for the side effects as well. This ought to be coupled with penalties for innovations that yield certain negative effects on life and society. This will likely increase the cost of innovation as well as the time for the concept to market. However, the long-term effect on health should outweigh the speed to market. Francois Rabelais once rightly said that *"Science without conscience is only ruin of the soul"*. Francois stated that science and technology are at the heart of people's lives and futures. It is in this light that innovators must take the ethical approach of innovation to account for the potential consequences of their design.

Innovation ethics should raise criteria for evaluation, it should show the ways to humanize innovation and increase moral imagination for innovation built around humans and societies. Given the present trends, this must include several sub-fields dealing with specific technological innovations (computer and information ethics, big data ethics, the ethics of block-chain, and others). It is only with this mindset that people can think more upstream, mitigate the drastic health and life effects of innovation. They certainly can chew the innovation gum while walking towards a truly enhanced quality of life.

\*\*\*\*\*\*\*\*\*\*\*\*\*\*\*\*\*\*\*\*\*\*\*\*\*\*\*\*\*\*\*\*\*\*\*\*

# Lesson 21

## SUMMARY

Smith proposed that "a nation's wealth should be judged by its total production and commerce", today known as the "Gross Domestic Product" (GDP) where GDP is an accurate indicator of the size of an economy. It was believed that sciences were the way to go if one wanted to change the world because Innovation was firmly linked to sciences and technology. However, a good mix of arts with the sciences in the African education system should be seriously considered as the way to go moving forward. Life expectancy can be increased or decreased depending on the part of town you live in. I still believe the COVID-19 pandemic is a blessing in disguise. Taking the lessons from this pandemic will enable the continent to prepare for the next one. All known futures markets are in industries that are organized vertically by specific products. This allows investment in specific crops like soybeans or oats. We would venture to say that with the preventive approach we end up with a healthier population and therefore fewer COVID-19 patients with underlying conditions resulting in fewer deaths.

Conclusively, this is perhaps the most ideal time for African countries to come up with the Infection "*Protection Act*" akin to the German version being modified to deal with COVID-19. The solution to the war with COVID-19 and future pandemics hinges on leveraging data and technology to complement the doctor's efforts. Barriers to success for girls need to be removed so they too can realize their fullest potential. I would like girls to be judged by the content of their character, by their competence and innate capabilities, and never at any point by their gender. Africa may be lacking in hard power, but the continent should take control of its soft power. The world ought to know more about the wit, courage, wisdom, and compassion of Africans. We must choose to make this goal our solemn mission. This decision should be made not because it is easy but rather because it is hard. It is the continental collective effort that will organize her citizens and bring forth the best of her skills and energies.

This is a challenge the continent must accept now and must be unwilling to postpone and must achieve. Artificial Intelligence has the extraordinary capacity to ceaselessly gain from and emphasize the information it gathers and moves organizations with the open doors it guarantees. The more information gathered and dissected, the more impressive the machine becomes, and the better people can work close by these machines. Conclusively, I stress the strength of the Diaspora because it is essential to the development of the continent.

African governments can no longer focus on geographical distance in the case of the Diaspora, meanwhile losing sight of the forest for the trees. There is not a better partner for economic and technological development today for Africa than her own

Diaspora. It is time to cut ties with old mindsets and wholeheartedly embrace her sons and daughters and work together as partners. It is now time for Africa to unleash its developmental secret weapon, its Diaspora.

African must shift focus to creating more adaptive governments as well as focusing on creating maximum value from a single transaction by using "Artificial Intelligence" (AI) and other technologies to best predict future needs and points of engagement. Companies must embrace risk to foster growth as well as providing the best value for the customers. Only in doing so will these companies keep up with or stay ahead of the competition. Blockchain is an exciting development that promises to change the way we live. As this piece of technology undergoes further progress, we will likely continue to see a growing list of potential use cases. Not all models are as accurate and a lot of advancements in the application of big data have tremendously increased the accuracy of these models.

Next-generation education will be completely transformed by AR/VR. This technology will empower students with holistic learning that adds on social, emotional, and creative components through intuitive experiences and simulations. It is estimated that by 2023, there will be a tremendous increase of AR devices from about 900 million today to almost 2.5 billion. AT&T is planning on utilizing its 5G technology to resolve medical challenges. Soon, we expect that robots will become more intelligent at performing various tasks. Even though this innovation can even now be considered as a beginning, its future is impressive.

By 2024, it is estimated that there will be more than $20 billion in IoT devices. By 2019 the market will increase to nearly 11.3 billion IoT devices. The future of IoT has a huge possibility of unfolding in the automotive industry. The right use and application of big data provides a competitive edge over your business counterparts. Technology is expanding with IA at the forefront. For now though AI and other technological advances are supporting the mental health field. Partnerships between emotion AI technology vendors and surveillance camera providers have emerged. Digital marketing professionals are leveraging the power of emotion detection to understand the emotions of their potential customers to improve customer experiences and to create a lasting bond. Emotion Recognition is improving our lives in many ways. It Is time for innovators to think upstream as they solve today's problems.

We are presently equipped with powerful analytical tools that if properly utilized will avert the adverse side effects of innovation to human life and ultimately the environment we live in. Innovation ethics should raise criteria for evaluation; it should show us ways to humanize innovation and increase moral imagination for innovation built around humans and societies. It is only with this mindset that we can think more upstream, mitigate the drastic health and life effects of innovation. We certainly can chew the innovation gum while walking towards a truly enhanced quality of life.

**\*\*\*\*\*\*\*\*\*\*\*\*\*\*\*\*\*\*\*\*\*\*\*\*\*\*\*\*\*\*\*\*\*\***

# CONCLUSION

At the end of this book, we conclude that if Africa wants to rise of poverty, it must understand how other countries are becoming rich. So, now we know that the secret to a country's wealth is its structure & system, geography, and its people. Most developed countries provide free or highly subsidized education as it enables people to use their talent to revolutionize many industries through technology and artificial intelligence and earn money. From this, we can understand that Africa needs to put a big chunk of money in investing in the education sector.

Africa's private sectors should be the driver of the innovative change while the government remain the enablers through creative adaptive governments as well as an appropriate allocation of resources. Business leaders and entrepreneurs should keep the focus on a few key consumer behaviors while driving massive personalization of products and services and focus on creating maximum value from a single transaction using artificial intelligence (AI) and other technologies to best predict future needs and points of engagement.

Governance and establishment should implement policies that foster economic growth. It should control corruption in the continent as Switzerland and Norway have been shown to do because when countries are corrupted, they face a double edge sword where they cannot collect enough taxes and with the little collected taxes, they cannot drive growth and reduce poverty. Also, with little taxes, the government cannot invest in important sectors such as education, health, and military security, etc.

With the use of the internet, Africa can be revolutionized as there is a large number of information stored on the internet, which can be used to make small changes and can contribute to growth. It is the responsibility of the whole nation to contribute to lifting the country's economy. Africa is rich in natural resources, therefore through using these, the continent can grow its economic level. Natural resources can enable Africa to become rich, while in the current situation the poor are getting poor and the rich are getting richer.

The Agriculture sector is the backbone of any country and it plays an important role in improving economic growth. Africa should adopt technology that increases agricultural productivity and the ability to amass wealth.

A country's wealth status is determined by its people as well. What the population thinks, feels, and believes makes a big difference in determining whether a country will be rich or not. When a country's people embrace innovations and think out of the box, it will invariably grow faster. If African people contribute their talent and aim high, then I believe that Africa can get out of poverty.

\*\*\*\*\*\*\*\*\*\*\*\*\*\*\*\*\*\*\*\*\*\*\*\*\*\*\*\*\*\*\*\*\*\*

www.ingramcontent.com/pod-product-compliance
Lightning Source LLC
Chambersburg PA
CBHW070552220526
45467CB00003B/1182